Rail
Special 3
Series Editor Tag Gorton

Ian Stock

THE ART OF GARDEN RAILWAYS

Reaching for Realism

Atlantic
PUBLISHERS

Front Cover –
A scene in 1950s Ireland – Cavan and Leitrim Number 8 – a modified
Archangel loco and scratch built West Clare diesel railcar number
3389 wait at Botar an Dunmore station. Photo: Neil Ramsay

Insets –
Left: *Taliesin* makes ready to depart from Castle Bryan on one of her
first revenue-earning trips since entering service. The management has
instituted a repair programme for the station; track renewals have already
taken place, and that delightfully decrepit station roof is also going to need
some attention ere long. The original operating plan did not anticipate the
ravages of a twenty-foot-high feline 'beast of Bryandale'... Adding the
structure to buildings like this gives wonderful opportunities for them
to decay gracefully and atmospherically. Photo: Ian Stock

Right: This Londonderry Loch Swilly 4-8-0 locomotive is a gas fired and
radio controlled model built by John Campbell and owned by David Mercer.
The train consists of Burtonport Extension coaches built by Neil Ramsay.
Photo: Neil Ramsay

Back Cover –
The two carriages seen here on the Hemlock Valley Railway are a couple
of GRS 'Lynton & Barnstaple' style kits weathered to simulate years of
wartime storage. Note the misted up windows and blinds of second-hand
green Barbour waterproof cotton. Photo: Paul Fletcher

Atlantic Publishers

83 Parkanaur Avenue, Southend-on-Sea, Essex SS1 3JA

ISBN: 978 1 902827 21 6

© Ian Stock

All rights reserved. No part of this publication may be reproduced, stored in
a retrieval system, or transmitted, in any form or by any means, electronic,
mechanical, photocopying, recording or otherwise, without prior permission
in writing from the publisher.

British Cataloguing in Publication Data
A catalogue for this book is available from the British Library

Layout and Production:
Juliet Arthur, Stimula Creative

Printed by Stephens & George, Merthyr Tydfil

Contents

Preface

By Tag Gorton

I DECIDED TO BUILD a garden railway comfortably over twenty years ago – and things were certainly a little bit different than they are nowadays. For a start, I knew of no one locally who had garden railway experience of any kind and so my initial planning of a steam powered 16mm scale narrow gauge railway was, of necessity, something of a shot in the dark. Certainly I picked up what I could from the rather erratically published *Steamlines* magazine and also from the quarterly *16mm Today* magazine, the house organ of the 16mm Narrow Gauge Modellers Association.

Both these sources of information were excellent for their time and I very much looked forward to each issue but, other than mining the information provided by authors who wrote about their own experiences and the very useful booklet provide by the 16mm Association, there was little I could do to avoid the several mistakes that I made on first constructing the embryo Longlands & Western Railway. The problem you see, is that one reads about what other people have done before subjecting the information to one's own critical analysis – and in my case I did not have the background information to do this properly.

The problem was that my analysis was based purely on how I imagined things would be, or would work, and my planning was done on rather this shaky foundation. Perhaps I can give you a 'f'rinstance.' As I gazed hungrily at the products of Roundhouse Engineering, Merlin Locomotive Works and Archangel Models within the pages of these early periodicals, I based my ideas on the only experience that I had – which was grounded, as you may imagine, on running indoor electric model railways. Now I am actually old enough to remember using clockwork Hornby trains on tracks that ran between chair and table legs in the dining room, and so, with this in mind, I most certainly did not want my first (and at this point 'only') steam locomotive to run without any sort of restraint. This seemed to me to be a step back into the dark ages and so radio control seemed the only way to go.

While undertaking this comparatively extensive period of armchair modelling, I would imagine just what it would be like to control a real 'live steam' locomotive, perhaps from the comfort of a deckchair on a sunny West Country afternoon, with the birds singing and the drowsy hum of insects providing a pleasurable descant to the busy chuff of my steam powered train. Well you see, after the first few 'training and experience' runs with my brand new radio controlled Merlin 'Mayflower' it didn't quite work out like that. I would find myself looking around for somewhere to put the radio control transmitter – or indeed at meetings I would hand it to someone who wanted to try out a locomotive. There were other problems. As I visited more and more lines I occasionally found (particularly with in situ rechargeable batteries) that I had accidentally left the thing switched on and my locomotive perforce had to remain a bench queen for the afternoon. The reality then, was that I was to find manual control of my locomotives to be preferable and I nowadays have only two steamers with fitted radio control.

PROSPECTIVE GARDEN RAILWAY

Coming from a background of indoor model railways, I had already determined that I wanted a railway running through a believable landscape. The simple 'tracks on sticks' running line was simply not for me because, apart from looking unsightly, it bore no relation all to a 'real' railway. Nowadays (and some twenty years older) I am very glad that the topography of my garden forced a section of my railway to be raised to a reasonable working height. I did stick to my principals however and raised the ground to meet the required height so that I could run in a scale environment. It was hard work to do, but one eventually reaches the stage where one blesses every inch off the ground!

Many people, when planning a garden railway for steam motive power, 'plan in' gradients, because they want to 'drive' their locomotives. Most, after a couple of years, wish that they had not done this. Different strokes for different folks of course – my way is most certainly not right for everyone or indeed for every prospective garden railway site. What I did find however, was that while my ever present and rose coloured imagination was taking me along paths that, in many cases I was going to regret – there were so many things I just never even thought about.

Which brings me to this book. A publication such as this would have been so helpful at the sort of pre-planning stage where imagination and proposed artistic endeavour have to be cross-referenced with practicality. What I did not need was a point-by-point listing of how to construct a garden railway in a particular way – after all I had my imagination and my reading to cope with that. I needed something to set my mind working and to ensure that I covered all the possibilities that were open to me. Ian Stock's book does just this. You may not agree with everything that he does or indeed, all that is covered herein – I don't myself. What this volume will do however – is to encourage innovative thinking about what you want from a prospective garden railway and how it can be created within the constraints that you have. Read the book – agree, disagree, ignore or take up each point or subject discussed by the author, but it will help you think about what you want to do with your hobby and your railway. Make your own decisions with this information in mind and you will eventually produce a railway that is not a clone of someone else's garden line, but something specifically yours that people will recognise as such…

IGOT INTO GARDEN RAILWAYS BY ACCIDENT – and I did it all wrong. Conventionally, you are meant to spend months pondering the shift in scale, doing amounts of detailed research, and above all going to lots of other garden railway 'meets' so that you know what you are letting yourself in for. You are meant to go in search of large lumps of metal to hew into a live steam locomotive with your bare hands. You are meant to work out in a gym for at least six months to toughen yourself up for mixing tonnes of concrete. And you are meant to own nothing smaller than a large paddock.

In my case, it was a spur-of-the-moment decision taken because I had no idea what else to do with the narrow strip of land down the side of our apartment. I won't grace it with the term 'garden'.

I had been aware of the existence of garden railways from my mid-Seventies' childhood reading of the articles of Dave Rowlands, Peter Denny and others in the 'Railway Modeller', and had long hankered to build something similar. However, I can honestly say that prior to that fateful day in September 2005, I had not given garden railways a thought for years, and I still cannot quite explain why the idea suddenly popped into my head. I suppose that mounting frustration with a severe lack of indoor modelling space was part of it – I was rapidly running out of steam with my third attempt to build something meaningful in the spare bedroom of our two-bedroom apartment, that would be satisfying to build and operate without completely incapacitating the room for its multitude of other necessary functions. It just wasn't working, and the

The LBR took a further leap forward in 2008 with the construction of Phase Three, which extended the line across the front of our property. The chance to build afresh allowed me to try out some of the ideas I had been developing in the interim. Here we see *Linda* rounding the bend where the new line deviated from the old, and heading for Minffordd (LBR) with a late afternoon train during the first autumn of this section's operation. There is still a great deal to be done on this stretch; the bridge, for example is due to be replaced with a double-arched steel structure from Keith Bucklitch. The enhanced appearance of the chaired track in the foreground is clearly visible.

thought of yet another round of baseboard building, track laying and wiring was not exactly enticing. Over the years, I had been moving slowly but steadily in the direction of fine scale modelling, but was becoming increasingly aware of a sense of frustration that models so detailed were becoming smaller and smaller in extent, little more than dioramas that (occasionally) moved. This not to deny that I am hugely inspired by the masters of fine scale modelling, and in fact the genesis of my thinking has been to try to embrace and adapt their philosophy to out of doors.

BLISSFULLY INNOCENT

And so the seed germinated; within a week, a length of Peco track appeared on what in my imagination was a track bed, 'just to get the idea'. My wife, having tentatively agreed to the principle of the thing, really had no idea what was about to

Above: I still don't know where the idea to put a garden railway in such a ridiculously small space came from. This picture shows that first length of track, laid using my 'patent' temporary track laying method outlined elsewhere. I have since regretted using that large gravel ballast, as the finer stuff I have since used just filters down through it, and has necessitated relaying the line on a new bed. However, I reckon if you can put a garden railway in a space like this, you can put one just about anywhere...

Left: The most unpromising site at the side of our property in early September 2005, before even I had any idea what was about to happen.

happen – but that length of track mysteriously sprouted another, and another, until there was something like a route disappearing into the undergrowth. Rapid clearance ensued of the builders' debris, abandoned estate agents' signs and ground elder that littered the site; my wife saw that, at least, as an improvement...

I decided that I had better do some planning, so a grand scheme was launched whereby the 40ft by 6ft (yes – *six*) plot would be transformed into a large and complex railway system, for that is what I had decided I was missing. And yet I was doing this without even having in my head a clear picture of the true size of the 16mm live steamers I proposed to use, never having actually seen one – let alone any idea how I was going to afford it. To say the least, I was blissfully innocent of the conventions and orthodoxy of the garden railway scene – and most of the practicalities too. Some of my ideas were quickly dismissed as unworkable, such as the proposed *underground* 2ft 6in radius return curve, and I came to the conclusion that an end-to-end U-shape was all that I would be able to achieve in the space. The fact that apparently flat ground is often nothing of the sort also did not really register until I started to calculate the likely gradients on a site that dropped about eighteen inches in its length. I realised that much more research was going to be necessary, and I should acknowledge the help and advice of Peter Hayward, one of my earliest email mentors in correcting me on some of the worst excesses of my earliest ignorance, while performing the delicate balancing act of tactfully not putting me off completely.

However, the point of the foregoing is this: despite my planning mistakes, I was able to put most of it right as I built, and most importantly of all, the weight of 'accepted practice' did not constrain me unduly. Online research provided some ideas, but a lot of it was developed as I went along. For instance, the fact that I did not even own the land (it is communally owned by all of the residents in our building) meant that I was reticent about laying track permanently, especially as I did not even know whether the model was going to be anything more

than a passing fad in a long line of such transient Stock undertakings. So I devised a method of fixing track in place without the need for sub-bases and major earthworks.

REALISTIC RAILWAY MODELLING

I was ignorant that conventional wisdom says live steamers really need a circuit – I didn't have much choice anyway – and I was blithely unaware that garden modelling was, in many ways, a completely different animal from indoor modelling made large. However, after four months' work, we made our way for the first time to PPS Models in Frome, parted with what seemed an inordinate amount of money for a 'toy' and had a working garden railway on our hands. And not only did it work, but it worked well. My increasing knowledge of the garden railway 'scene' was indicating that such models simply would not be rewarding or reliable working a 100ft end to end line with steep gradients and tight bends, but nonetheless, work it did. What is more, it gradually began to dawn on me just what potential the great outdoors offered for realistic railway modelling. Many of the problems faced by indoor modellers were simply absent – lighting was no problem, colours were natural, weathering happened automatically, and bizarrely, despite the incongruities of scale, it seemed possible to create a highly convincing model railway in this way.

However, I was also becoming increasingly bemused by those 'conventional wisdoms' of garden railway modelling; coming from an indoor modelling background, the priorities of the model engineering part of the community were hard for me to come to terms with. I saw some magnificent machinery that had clearly been crafted by people with skills totally alien to me, but I could not understand why they wished to run them on tracks elevated on posts, and why many ran few or no other vehicles behind them. I could not understand why some such models were run on lines with little or no other railway infrastructure, and I found the widespread acceptance of the 'six

Above: The same train, seen a little later calling at Minffordd. The name may be clichéd, but once I discovered that it means 'Side of the Road' in Welsh, no other name would do. A lot of the inspiration here came from the Ffestiniog Railway, and was starting to prove my ideas about the feasibility of prototype-based models. I was very pleased with the way in which the general atmosphere was developing, given that the station had been in existence for little more than nine months.

Right: Stations benefit from being given space to breathe. This is essential if one wants to recreate the uncluttered effect of many rural narrow-gauge lines. This can often be created in the most unlikely sites.

foot rule' (i.e. if it looks O.K. from a distance then that will do) at odds with what was rapidly becoming for me a key attraction of the larger scale, namely to opportunity to increase the fidelity and detail of my models still further. The view that fine detail just does not survive out of doors was not what I was finding at all.

I should emphasise at this point that I mean no criticism of those who choose such an approach for their hobby – after all, this is *only* a hobby, and if we cannot be free to do our own thing in that at least, it is a poor state of affairs. However, my instincts were all telling me that there were more, or at least different opportunities to be had from another approach. The point I am making is that every hobby has its collective wisdom,

and in many cases it can be very useful – after all, there are many who have gone before us, and the problems they encountered may well be little different from the ones that we come to anew. However, there are also times when orthodoxy can become a straightjacket, either because times, conditions, expectations or technology have changed, or because 'known facts' turn out to be rather less fact and rather more a collection of personal superstition. I wonder how many people over the years have been bound by certain ways of doing something not because it is the best solution but simply because it has become the *accepted* way of doing it.

ENTRENCHED PERCEPTION

Within the wider railway modelling world, garden modellers seem to be viewed with some curiosity; they also seem to have acquired a reputation of being the mavericks of the hobby, those who have sought refuge from the larger and perhaps

Above: Another of those shots that just makes you want to get out there and do more. *Linda* shunting slate wagons on the quay at Port Penrhyn - sorry – Tarren Hendre…

Left: Barely any railway in this view of Tarren Hendre's wharf, but it all lends plausibility to the overall scene, and experience of being there.
Photo: Sara Stock

coloured, mis-proportioned buildings; rolling stock was determinedly eccentric, made from discarded margarine tubs and the like by people who appeared to take active pride in their lack of finer skills. In short, I seemed to have stumbled on the one area of railway modelling that gave not two hoots whether the results bore much resemblance to the real railway.

Running one's railway was mostly a matter of chasing one's tail round in never-ending circles until the gas ran out, especially at garden railway meets, those most sociable of model railway events – where in fact most people seem determined to cooperate with their fellow to no greater extent than that required to prevent an almighty pile-up of their beloved contraptions. What is more, the sociability did not particularly seem to extend to members of other 'clans' of outdoor modeller, and most definitely NOT to indoor modellers, of whose ways a surprising number of my new colleagues appeared blissfully ignorant. For all the talk of tolerance, there appeared to be a surprising amount of unspoken rivalry. But above all, garden railways were not meant to be realistic, serious attempts to recreate the real railway – as we all know, that simply isn't possible in a garden.

THINK THE UNTHINKABLE

Before I am accused of being an intolerable snob, let me say that I am over-stating the caricature for the sake of the argument, and as time has moved on I have understood more of where the outlook has come from. I have also found a set of friends who have enriched my wider life, even though some of them perhaps privately hold as many reservations about my approach as I sometimes do about theirs. I hope they don't mind my poking a little fun at them for the sake of this book; their friendship, I know, is real.

However, an amount of heart-searching told me that it was ridiculous to consider dropping something that I was greatly

more homogenous scene of the 'indoors' brigade. In the case of those modelling on the narrow gauge, this has perhaps been compounded by the other entrenched perception that NG modelling is not 'serious' in the way that standard gauge modelling is. All those 009 'rabbit warren' layouts of the 1970s did nothing to help dispel this view, and within the outdoors scene, isn't NG what those who have not the skill or money to run G1 do?

I will confess that about a year into my project, I began to have second thoughts, not because I was not enjoying what I was doing, but because my growing knowledge of the wider garden railway scene was telling me that I was trying to break too many rules. Garden railways were always tongue in cheek; they were populated by cartoon characters who lived in garishly

Late afternoon, and the Railway's latest acquisition, single Fairlie *Taliesin*, awaits the guard's whistle before picking her way gingerly over the newly re-laid track in the station throat, and heading off along the valley with a train for Queen's Forest Road. The first section will be easy, as it is downhill most of the way to Minffordd, but then the fireman will be in for some hard slog… The Railway tries to keep its rolling stock looking presentable, but coach Nº4 looks as though it will need a visit to the works before too long.

enjoying simply due to imagined peer pressure, and I decided to press on. My new resolve was helped by my widening electronic contacts with people such as Neil Ramsay, Paul Sherwood, David Rowbotham, David Halfpenny and Jeremy Ledger whose philosophy appeared much closer to my own, and whose work has been a constant source of inspiration and challenge. I was reassured that it was possible to think the unthinkable and aim to create something more than a model engineer's test track in one's garden.

And so to the aim of this book: to reconsider some of those orthodoxies in the light of the growing and developing interest in garden railways, to stimulate some debate about what can or might be achieved, and hopefully to encourage others who might be unsure of the medium to take the plunge into the wonderful world of full-on outdoor garden railway modelling.

NARROW GAUGE RAILWAYS have long suffered from an unfortunate image, even amongst railway enthusiasts. I suppose it is the perceived eccentricity, the devil-may-care attitude to convention and above all the sometimes toy-like appearance of the trains that has done it – and I am talking about the prototype here! There is at least one mid twentieth-century photographer on record as saying that he did not care to photograph the Festiniog Railway because there was far too much of interest on the nearby standard gauge lines.

In short, the Narrow Gauge railways are not to be taken too seriously – they are at best a humorous if charming diversion from the serious stuff of the standard gauge – and we modellers have tended to swallow this outlook hook, line and sinker. Narrow Gauge models do not run well (or so people think), and they tend to be modelled in unconvincing ways for a bit of fun by those whose serious interest lies elsewhere. In recent years, there have been a few brave individuals such as Peter Kazer and Paul Holmes, whose respective models of Corris and Borth y Gest have derived from fine scale practice, and who have argued that the narrow gauge is worthy of serious study and modelling in their own right. However, their thinking remains that of a small, if growing minority.

SLIGHTLY ECCENTRIC

And who am I to evangelise? For many years, my own interest in narrow gauge lines could best be euphemistically described as 'dormant', and indeed, my residual indoor modelling remains on the standard gauge, even if my outdoor activities have moved me in the direction of rather more off-beat proto-types. Yet this is not to deny that my fascination in the narrow gauge is real – it is just that it has taken garden modelling for it to find its best outlet, for there is an indefinable 'something' about the smaller trains that, practical considerations apart, seems to make them sit more easily in the garden environment than standard gauge models. There are some truly impressive

I don't care what the public thinks about railway enthusiasts – I challenge anyone to stand on the sea wall at Porthmadog with a line-up like this in front of them, and not be enthused. I am pretty sure that not all of the people busy snapping away that morning in 2006, were enthusiasts. These small locomotives seem able to pack in charm, power, approachability and a certain elegance into their small proportions – and we can have it all again in our gardens...

garden main lines to be seen in gauges 0 and 1, but almost without exception they are model railways built in a garden, rather than garden railways in the more subtle sense – and they tend to dominate rather than integrate with their surroundings.

Certainly, amongst the wider garden narrow gauge railway fraternity, it is the lighter-hearted approach that predominates – and why not, if that is where the majority interest lies? Why shouldn't the Seven Dwarves turn up on your station platform if you so choose? After all, we are talking about nothing more than a slightly (?) eccentric hobby here – and if one cannot pursue at least one's hobby utterly in the way one chooses, then what is the point of it? Yet, as I said in the Introduction, such an outlook still manages to foster its own orthodoxy, its own blinkered views, even a degree of cussedness – sometimes to the point of masking the excellence of the workmanship – which can be quite off-putting to the newcomer who may come from a very different background, and be in search of something different.

To be a 'serious' garden modeller of narrow-gauge practice is, apparently, a double contradiction in terms. However, I would argue that there is some confused thinking going on

> *To be able to fill leisure intelligently is the last product of civilisation, and at present very few people have reached this level...*
>
> Bertrand Russell

Top right: Proof that our models can draw the crowds in pretty much the same way. I think the key is to create something so engaging that people are sufficiently intrigued by what is going on that they are drawn into the model. The key ingredients for doing that are quality and character. The 2008 Open Gardens weekend in our village drew a healthy audience for the Lower Bryandale Railway. We have had to get used to running in public, but the feedback has been more than worth it, both for its own sake, and for the opportunities for reflection that the showmanship created. *Photo: Sara Stock*

Centre: The small size of narrow gauge trains undoubtedly adds to their appeal – they are less remote and overwhelming than main line locomotives. However, we often tend to forget the true relationship between our models and the real thing. The true proportions of *Edward Thomas* are apparent in this view of a Talyllyn train waiting to leave Tywyn Wharf.

Lower: Even a small prototype station would require a large space in 16mm scale. This is Woody Bay on the re-opened Lynton & Barnstaple Railway – hardly large, but it would still require something over thirty feet to model it to full scale.

here: to take one's hobby 'too' seriously does not imply that one has to take *oneself* 'too' seriously. In the greater scheme of things, the outcome of our modelling activities is not going to make or break world peace; but the same could be said of many other aspects of human endeavour. One would probably not expect, say, an amateur musical instrument maker, artist or sportsman *not* set themselves reasonably 'serious' targets. This does not however, mean that they would need to lose their sense of humour or proportion in the process. Perhaps the self-effacing approach of our hobby, actually stems from a subconscious awareness that we are too easily ridiculed as grown adults playing with toys – with all the social overtones that such an opinion can carry and, as yet, garden railways are not an Olympic sport.

KNOWLEDGE, SKILL AND PATIENCE

I think it is fair to say that this stigma afflicts the railway enthusiast community as a whole – just think of the negative associations in the media and wider society of the term 'train-spotter' (which is generally used to mean all railway enthusiasts) to see what I mean. In the case of garden railways, we also risk association with the devotees of garden gnomes and other such tweeness – which is perhaps even more socially doubtful than are railway enthusiasts. However, it need not be like this. I challenge anyone to undermine the credentials of the grand old men of railway enthusiasm – the likes of OS Nock, Ivo Peters and James Boyd – and there is nothing inherently deficient about having an interest in railways – you can even do a degree in it…

For us more ordinary mortals, the answer perhaps lies in being clear on the difference between 'toy' and 'model' and ensuring that our level of excellence matches that seen in other, more acceptable hobbies. In my own experience, many non-enthusiasts actually admire the knowledge, skill and patience required by high-quality model making. My Lower Bryandale Railway is necessarily on full public view, but much to my surprise many of my neighbours have reacted not with the anticipated condescension to the sight of a grown, professional man 'playing' with small steam trains but instead with genuine, if slightly amused interest.

The reaction of the non-railway public can be very instructive. It is possible to see live steam trains running on portable layouts at exhibitions, but while there are other examples of front gardens being used for lines, for obvious reasons, this is comparatively rare; I however, had no choice. Consequently, over the past five

years I have been able to conduct a fascinating social experiment: because I had to work so largely in the public view, I ended up doing the one thing that is impossible for most garden railway modellers, namely exhibiting my model. The upshot of this is that I have spent a lot of time observing and learning from the reactions of lay-viewers in terms of what arouses their curiosity and interest. Fortunately, they have been too polite to show any negative reactions, but the most interesting thing of all was that the trains have appealed to almost everyone. The only group whom I have yet to dent is the older teenage girls… It is nonetheless gratifying and encouraging to hear not infrequently, a teenage voice squealing, "How cool is *that*?" as they catch sight of the railway. So we can rejoice in the fact that, despite my earlier comments, our hobby is now the height of Cool…

THE 'CUDDLY' IMAGE

More seriously, I am fortunate to live in an area sufficiently benign for the railway to receive a positive response; regrettably, there may be more areas of the UK where this would probably not be the case, and it is not through needless paranoia that most modellers do not advertise the presence of their railways. What is more, many people wish to enjoy their lines in privacy, rather than involuntarily share them with all-comers. Most modellers are motivated primarily by internal factors, and as such they are really only concerned with their own rewards, but I suspect that this sometimes works to their own detriment. The forced experience of interacting with other people over the railway on a daily basis has provided much food for thought; it has led me to consider what makes a successful garden railway,

and while the answer ultimately has to be 'one that pleases its creator', we can perhaps learn more than we care to admit from others' reactions to what we do. In the process, not only may we please those around us, but we may find that giving more consideration to the wider aspects of our hobby actually brings us more satisfaction too.

In the battle to gain wider acceptance for our activities, it seems that the general public's love of trains is a major weapon in our armoury, if only it can be tapped into successfully. The Railway, it seems, is embedded in our culture in a way that no other form of transport can match, and nearly everyone is able to relate what they are seeing to some experience of their own. On this front, the 'cuddly' image of narrow gauge railways can only add further to our advantage, as they seem to fit so easily into the garden setting.

I hope that readers will forgive me this digression into Sociology – like most, in the final reckoning no amount of social disapprobation would make me give up my hobby! However, it is perhaps a relevant consideration in terms of the impact it has on how we go about doing what we do with our own small empires, and it is perhaps less surprising if we encounter opposition or even ridicule from others if we exhibit no awareness of

The Maesffordd & Nant Gorris Railway is a line with a strong Welsh character, despite its actual location in East Anglia. Here we see one of the stalwarts of the line, Nº3 *Dilys* awaiting her next turn of duty at Portcoed, the main station on the line. Paul Sherwood was one of the first to demonstrate the potential for creating a complete railway setting out of doors, and he has become expert in the process. Photo: Paul Sherwood

Left: While on the subject of proportions, just look at the impact of these scale-sized buildings on Andrew Crookell's new line. They may only be cardboard mock-ups at this stage, but they have been taken accurately from photographs of real slate quarry originals. They tower over the trains in the way many proprietary models just don't, and in the process re-emphasise the true largeness of our models. And in doing so, they certainly add to the atmosphere…

Centre: Large buildings such as this working watermill on Tarren Hendre can serve as usual view blockers, and can be contrived as exits for tracks going off-stage. As in this case, they can also be appealing diversions in their own right. Photo: Andrew Crookell

Right: The wisdom that you cannot model to high levels of detail out of doors is being called more and more into question, and this picture of a station on Bill Winter's Llyfni Vale line is surely all the evidence needed. What is true, however, is that structures out of doors will need more maintenance than their indoor counterparts – but then so do real buildings. Bill makes all of the 'incidentals' such as the bicycle from scratch, and just look at the result. Notice, too, that tremendously convincing ground surface. Photo: Richard Stallwood

our relationship with the wider world. In line with the unexpected scale of our models, perhaps our own sense of proportion is in need of some readjustment if we are to realise the full potential of what we do.

THE DEGREE OF SKILL

There is nothing 'sad' about having a hobby, despite the fact that with the contemporary pressures on the work-life balance, the cost of living and increasing numbers of more passive alternatives, perhaps fewer people are actively pursuing them. In fact, within the realm of the 'skilled amateur' lies a considerable amount of this and every other nation's 'cultural capital'; belonging to a choral society or a golf club, collecting wine or restoring old sports cars are regarded as perfectly reasonable things to do, though of course like everything else (at least in British society) all such activities come with their own bag of gender, social and economic connotations. Many people in many areas of amateur life attain very high levels of excellence. Model making is not inherently an 'unrespectable' activity either, when one thinks about the prices that vintage models now fetch at auction, the fact that museums and architects have always relied on fine model-making for educational or informational reasons, and the number of homes around the world that must be graced for

decorative or sentimental purposes with 'miniatures' of one kind or another.

What perhaps makes a difference is the degree of skill and application that the individual applies to what they are doing. Many great things have been achieved by people working in the voluntary sector; great art collections have been amassed by people doing it basically for the love of it, and even within our own field, just consider the very real benefits that railway preservation is now bringing to the economic fortunes of certain parts of our country. However, like most things, 'It's not what you do, it's the way that you do it' that makes the critical difference – and perhaps there are times when as a movement, railway enthusiasts *do* invite the ridicule of others. I wonder whether the reaction to my own railway would have been different had it consisted solely of off-the-shelf commercial products rather than largely self-made items, and if I had not imposed the self-discipline of strict quality control on what I put out there.

Some may accuse me of over-intellectualising what is basically 'a bit of fun'; well perhaps, but 'fun' comes in all shapes and sizes. As with all hobbies, railways can be enjoyed at numerous levels, and I am certainly not trying to claim that one approach is inherently superior to another. Given the pressures of modern life, it seems perfectly reasonable to me that many people, maybe even the majority, will be looking to purchase off-the-shelf models to run in their gardens precisely to have 'a bit of fun' without making the significant investment of the time that they may not in any case have in our cash-rich, time-poor society. Personally, however, I have always sought something else from my leisure activities. While enjoyment is of course the primary goal, I do believe that hobbies can add more to one's life than a perhaps rather transient bit of fun; one's working life may be essential in order to feed the body, but what one does the rest of the time can be just as important when it comes to feeding the soul! Perhaps my profession as a teacher is speaking more strongly here than I care to admit, but I look for two main rewards from a hobby: the personal creative challenge of producing the most finely-crafted models of which I am capable, and a vehicle for the greater understanding and expression of my fascination with the subject that binds us all in the first place: the railway.

DIMENSIONS OF FIDELITY

While my move from small to large scale models was apparently a chance event, there were no doubt underlying thoughts at work. Firstly, my recent involvement in the railway preservation movement was leading to a greater appreciation of the nature of the real thing, and this was creating some frustration with the

Neil Ramsay makes the most exquisite models of Irish 3ft gauge stock. This particular item is a brake van from the Lough Swilly line. A single item of rolling stock can take him in excess of two hundred hours, and it has become the primary focus of his hobby activity. These museum-quality models most definitely do earn their living on his garden railway, but in my opinion, the craftsmanship involved can easily hold a torch to that admired in other fine, craft-based undertakings. Photo: Neil Ramsay

limitations of small scale models; this in turn was being compounded by that extreme shortage of indoor space in which to create a meaningful model, even in our fairly large apartment. Secondly, as a result I was moving up in scale because I wished to produce more realistic models than the small scales made possible without the use of a micrometer and magnifier, and thirdly, the 'bug' of live steam was biting stronger as a result of more frequent brushes with full sized locomotives.

The move itself may have been a random event, but it did not take me long to appreciate just how much closer to the real thing a garden railway potentially can be than even the finest indoor model. To begin with, one may be able to consider building something that approximates to an entire railway, even if significantly shortened, and this is of course assisted by the self-contained nature of narrow gauge prototypes. As a result one can, oneself, become part of the scene, run it from within and view it from a multitude of viewpoints, rather than remain a detached observer, fated forever to look inward on one's model from the edge of a baseboard. This is a particular problem with modern indoor layouts which thanks to the decreasing size of modern homes are becoming smaller and smaller affairs, in many cases little more than very fine dioramas – and I suspect that it is the root of the dissatisfaction that sees many people building a series of short-term layouts rather than working on a single project over a longer period; I for one was tired of doing just that.

To such considerations, one can add the extra dimensions of fidelity that large-scale models present. One has to build with much more respect for the forces that apply in real life, and thus the process of creating one's model becomes part of the realism, rather than simply a means to an end. The large size of the items means that 'material fidelity' becomes a more viable proposition. As time has gone on, I have become more and more an advocate of a 'ban the plastic' philosophy. Wood should be represented only by wood, metal by metal, glass by glass and so on; in this way, the material qualities of the real thing are most effectively portrayed, and I now only use plastic as a last resort when I cannot source or work with a more authentic alternative. While the motivation for doing this was mostly internal, it did have significant external effect.

AUTHENTIC NATURAL MATERIALS

Given its situation, my railway was always going to have an impact on many other people. For this reason, I also had to give

considerable thought to what my neighbours would find acceptable on what was, after all, communal land. I felt that the models needed, by general consensus, to enhance the property rather than detract from it – and given that, I concluded that the most sure-fire way of doing the latter would have been to land a lot of artificial-looking, brightly coloured features into what is basically a small front garden, and end up with the railway equivalent of garden-gnome land. Authentic, natural materials have allowed me instead to create something that has blended in well, the textures and colours remaining subdued, and the overall effect being something closer to a natural-looking landscape garden than a toyshop.

In addition to the possibilities for improving the models' visual fidelity, garden railways also present other dimensions of realism. The most notable, of course, is that of sound. A garden-size live steamer makes many of the same sounds as a full sized locomotive, and to that I suppose we should also add smells. When they run, the move with a gait and momentum much closer to the real thing than does something with less heft, while the sound or wheel on rail is correspondingly louder and more convincing, especially if one arranges one's rail joints appropriately.

The fact that the garden railway normally remains out of doors permanently, subject to changes in season, weather and light adds incrementally to a much more intense experience than anything that has to be packed away or left out of sight in the loft for much of the time. The railway assumes a life of its own, and even when the trains are not running it pulls you into its world. Every morning, as I leave for work I pass the line, rails shining in the morning sun, or overnight rain gradually drying on the platform, while I am greeted by it as the first thing I see on my return in the evening, the light and atmosphere having changed completely during the day. And then, when the trains are running, there is that same *frisson* that you experience on discovering an active full-size operation, in my case often shared by the passers-by, especially the children whose shouts of excitement signify their anticipation at actually seeing a train. How much more realism do you need?

CONVENTIONAL GARDEN RAILWAYS

And let's not forget that garden railway scales are big: a forty-foot long coach reduced to one nineteenth scale is still a large object, and while the general appeal of models is undoubtedly in their smallness, big models ironically command far more 'presence' than something that could have been made by a watch-maker. Even quite small garden railways occupy spaces that would be the envy of those indoors, but if anything, we suffer even more from an acute lack of the stuff. Just consider this: were one to build a true-scale model of the entire Lynton & Barnstaple Railway at 1:19, it would still be one real mile long, and rise to a height of *fifty* feet. The terminus station at Lynton would occupy a space nearing fifty feet long, more than some of us have for our entire railways! Even the rather shorter Talyllyn Railway would still be nearly half a mile long if modelled in its entirety. While even contemplating such a task is somewhat ridiculous, it does serve to illustrate a point – most of us build our railways on a space more appropriate for a model fairground ride. If we then reinforce that fact by using track

that also appears to have come from that source, it is perhaps not surprising that so many conventional garden railways end up looking not entirely unlike one.

Perhaps one of the reasons that we still get this perception so wrong is that the blurring of scale caused by putting a model into a full-sized landscape confuses us. Many uninitiated people who see my line for the first time assume that it is 'O' gauge standard gauge, despite the proportions of some of the surrounding structures. I even found myself making the same false assumption when working on the line – somehow I still mentally reference proportions from standard gauge track, and hence I tend to under-estimate the true largeness of my chosen scale. After all, SM32 track appears reasonably sizeable even in the garden, but when one remembers just how small real-life 2ft gauge track is, one is forced to re-think that relationship.

The first time this became apparent was when I added some scale-height telegraph poles to my line – apart from other visual benefits discussed later, they immediately redefined the scale of the track in relation to the surroundings; a simple but effective trick. During 2008, I added an extension to my Lower Bryandale Railway, some three years after starting the original. In the interim, my thinking and experience had developed considerably, and I was determined to try out many new ideas. By this time I was mindful of this pitfall, but I still managed to underestimate the eventual impact of the railway on the space at my disposal. If we do this on a regular basis while planning and constructing our models, we risk totally miscalculating the visual effect that we will end up with – loops too short, platforms too narrow, sidings too short etc., if one relies on the track gauge as an

indicator of other key dimensions. I now always keep at least one item of rolling stock, usually a long bogie coach, with me during all periods of significant planning and construction to act as a constant reminder of the scale of the finished model.

DEGREE OF COMPRESSION

The ridiculous degree of compression that most of us work with might seem to torpedo the notion of achieving a realistic-looking railway before we have started, yet it is something that indoor modellers have of course been dealing with as well for decades; the difference is perhaps that they, being more inclined to try to recreate something visually very close to the real railway, and having fewer distractions on their bare baseboards, had to find solutions longer ago. We can take comfort from the fact that so many models succeed on this front despite still being massively compressed, and more from our advantage that narrow gauge lines were mostly smaller and more variable in size than their standard gauge counterparts to begin with. The practical implications of this issue are discussed later, but suffice it to say at this stage that we need to be aware of the issues in the early stages of developing our models if we are to resolve the problems satisfactorily.

Another surprise that lurked waiting me in the early days was the Six Foot Rule. This generally dictates more or less tongue-in-cheek that anything not visible from six feet away is not worth modelling, and will probably not be visible in the garden context anyway. While this is no doubt very helpful in reducing the complexity, timescale and required skill levels of the models we make, it can also produce some very crude results, devoid of the very character and atmosphere that I believe is essential. Like it or not, this will communicate quite clearly the approach of the builder. Of course, individuals will judge what meets their own requirements, and I suppose the philosophy is no different from that in aero-modelling where many models are purely functional 'semi-scale models' which fly well (probably better than highly detailed ones) and from several hundred feet below look acceptable. But fine-scale models

Neil Ramsay may be best interested in building rolling stock, but this has not stopped him from putting considerable thought into creating a convincing environment in which they can be run. Here we see the goods transhipment facilities at the long station of his line in Herefordshire. Note the massive proportions of the Irish Standard Gauge (5ft 3in gauge) wagon on the left – built by Neil to re-emphasise the contrast with the smaller 3ft gauge stock. Photo: Neil Ramsay

Above: Minffordd (LBR) in the morning sun, as seen when leaving for work each morning. The perpetual presence of a garden railway, living along side you in real time and space makes for the most intensively real of model experiences I have yet encountered – or am likely to.

Left: One of the best uses of real topography that I have seen is on Dave Mees' Wigfa & Llanrwst Railway in North Wales. Not only does he have an authentic climate for his line (!) but the site of his home necessitated the bridging of this gully at two points during the line's construction. Dave has built some superb bridges including this copy of one near Blaenau Ffestiniog. It needs to be able to withstand a spate of up to a couple of feet deep. What a wonderful real backdrop Dave has for his line – no contrived artistry needed!

painstakingly researched and made, worthy of close inspection, and loaded with the atmosphere of the original, they are not. Similar railway models will happily trundle along behind a live-steamer or battery loco, providing a payload and adding the semblance of a train, but to my eye, that is about it. They look too much like toys, devoid of too many references to the real railway – and in my opinion they represent a massive missed opportunity. The growth of interest in 'O' Gauge and larger on the indoor scene has been sparked partly by the increasing age of a generation of modellers who are increasingly struggling to cope with microscopic detail, and also the renewed appreciation that these large models somehow capture more of the feel of the real thing than those which are effectively viewed from several hundred yards away.

DETAIL AND AUTHENTICITY

Some of the most masterful indoor layouts of recent years have been in the 'senior scales'; I am thinking of the likes of Inkerman Street, East Dean and Martyn Welch's Hursley. So why is it that we, who have the largest scale of all to work with, see it as an opportunity to *reduce* detail rather than revel in it? Admittedly, with increasing scale, the locomotives increasingly take centre-stage as the space for ancillary items decreases, but why do even the trains running behind them often seem like an after-thought? Large-scale modelling allows me to further one of my two stated aims – to increase the detail and authenticity

of my models without having to rely on an Optivisor to make and appreciate my work. In the larger scales, the construction of an individual item is itself much more of an undertaking (another gain in process-realism), the final model potentially far more an item of character and beauty in its own right – but *we* then have the luxury of taking such items and making them part of something still more magical in our gardens…

In this chapter, I have tried to suggest that the wider context within which we conduct our hobby, and the expectations that we (and others) have of what we are doing, will fundamentally shape the outcome. Conventionally, garden railways have maintained an esoteric and rather reductivist relationship with the wider world, and this has perhaps contributed to both a degree of prejudice on the part of those outside the hobby and some entrenched thinking within it.

As the modern hobby of garden railways develops and more newcomers enter the hobby, it is inevitable that the number of approaches and expectations will multiply. Alongside the mainstream interest in engineering, there should be room for a more realistic, finer approach to what we do, which encompasses the entire railway environment and is at least as interested in scenery, gardening and architecture as the trains themselves; it may be more of a modelling-led approach than is traditional – experience is starting to show that the rough-and-tumble of the outdoors need not be the impediment that conventional wisdom suggests, and that there is the scope for the creation of something quite amazing.

T HAT INITIAL RUSH OF ENTHUSIASM can be a powerful thing. If you are the kind of person who relishes having a new project, the imperative to get going is sometimes almost irresistible, and I suspect that many railway enthusiasts, by virtue of being the kind of people who have strong hobby passions, are some such.

I have never really worked out just what it is about railways that generates such fascination, and perhaps it is better not to try too hard. Moreover, I can see no clear link between admiring a hundred-tonne leviathan, and wishing to replicate it (in what will inevitably be an emasculated way) in miniature; there are many railway enthusiasts who have no desire whatsoever to make models - but most people do seem to find some way of mediating their interest in what would otherwise be a passive, observational experience of just watching trains go by.

Be that as it may, I have made model railways for as long as I can remember – a train set was the only plaything I really needed as a child. The question, 'Why?' simply never came into it, and it is only recently, with my increasing focus on the theoretical aspects of railway modelling, that I have begun to ruminate on the fundamental motivations behind what we do.

Perhaps a more satisfactory answer can be found by looking upon modelling as a form of self-expression, a way of recording our memories and experiences of the real thing – which takes

My 'Linda' passing through Shade Gap station on Andrew Coward's line. Andrew's use of vegetation has been so successful that one instantly forgets that this was built in an average-sized suburban garden.

Left: It is shots like this that helped to raise my sights in terms of what might be achievable on a garden railway. There is not even a train in sight (which is perhaps symptomatic of my approach), but this slate wall, built from the real stuff by Laurie Wright, is so achingly close to the real thing that one is momentarily fooled. Notice how a mundane structure has just been so well observed that it captures the essence of the real thing, as observed alongside narrow gauge railways all over the principality; in my opinion this is just as important for the overall effect as the trains themselves. And just look at the quality of track bed and weathering, provided gratis by Mother Nature, once the initial possibility had been created...

Opposite top: Having been inspired by Laurie and others, I began to feel that I was perhaps getting somewhere when I saw this photo of my new station. The textures are beginning to look pleasing, even if the weathering needs more time to mature. I am also beginning to see the possibilities for 'artful' shots of the railway, as opposed to a simple documentary style.

Opposite lower: Further encouragement came from this shot of *Linda* rounding the bend where Phase 3 adjoins Phase 2. The original line used to curve left at this point over the original Glen Olibhe Viaduct, now relocated further down the valley.

us dangerously close to the 'A' word – Art. Whether it is the mechanical tinkering that people enjoy, or something more impressionistic, there is no doubt that railways stir emotions in people, and it seems that we need to find a way of reflecting that. Some people get involved with running the real thing; others choose to photograph railways, while we recreate them in miniature, and of course, conveniently iron out the less-than-perfect bits on the way – which, by some measures, is a definition of Art.

HISSED, SWEATED AND CLANKED

As I said earlier, my move into garden railways was, on the face of it an almost random event, but I do recall the one thing that was the driving imperative – the desire to own and run a steam locomotive that roared, hissed, sweated and clanked like the real thing; quite why I needed to own one, I can't be sure; perhaps it gave me unlimited dominion over what these days is otherwise a fairly infrequent experience. Having moved increasingly from diesel modelling to steam, purely on the grounds that steam-era railways seemed to have more modelling potential, I found that I had been crept up on and mugged by the fascination of steam itself. Unlike many older modellers, I cannot claim that it is

nostalgia, for I am somewhat too young to remember steam on the main line, and it is also quite out of character since in most matters, my tastes are distinctly modernist. But nonetheless, all of a sudden, electric models of steam trains just would not do – and that meant going up several scales, and also looking for somewhere else to run them...

The relevance of this navel-gazing lies in the fact that by understanding at least some of what motivates us in our hobby, we may be more likely to achieve a satisfactory and fulfilling outcome. While I previously made a virtue of my ad-lib entry into the hobby, it might have been easier to have stopped and considered what I really wanted to achieve; other than the live steam aspect, I had very few focussed ideas about it, although I was clear about what I did not want, namely a garden model village, which I rightly or wrongly considered to be rather naff. I will hasten to say, though, that this view has been modified quite considerably in the interim – which is what the rest of this book is about!

It did not take me long to discover that the garden railway world is a far more eclectic one than that of indoor modelling. The latter tends to divide between those who basically want a train set to play with, and the majority who, to the best of their ability, are trying to replicate real railway scenarios in miniature.

I counted myself very much in the latter camp, and it came as quite a shock, on moving outdoors, to encounter people whose concepts of realism were not only wildly different from mine, but who did not necessarily consider that realism, in the modelled sense, was a particularly important objective in the first place.

FULL-ON GARDEN MODEL

Garden railway modelling is an older hobby than its indoor counterpart, and it was a rich man's plaything, long before technology made possible smaller and smaller mass-produced models, moving the hobby indoors and democratisating it in the process. However, in the meantime, garden railways seem to me to have got stuck in something of a time-warp, and it has only been in the last few years that commercial and now creative thinking has started to move on, fuelled no doubt by those who now have the means to explore their potential.

It is also clear that the creation of a garden railway is a significantly larger undertaking than is an indoor one; materials and components – to say nothing of complete trains – are expensive; the quantities and types of material required are greater and harder to work; the physical task of building the railway is more demanding – and there is much more on-going maintenance required. Building a full-on garden model is a demanding task, and it is perhaps this that has led to the various compromise situations that seem to exist, and which neatly sum up the different aims that one might have in building the thing in the first place:

1. The model engineer's 'test track'. This is the most traditional form of garden railway; the trains are almost exclusively the focus of activity, not least because they are often engineered from scratch, and the railway needs to be little more than a suitable length of track on which such models can be enjoyed. Little thought tends to be given to the wider railway infrastructure, let alone what lies outside the boundary fence. Lines are usually built raised on posts for ease of use and viewing.

2. A smaller number of railways that are basically extensions of indoor models, used to provide a lengthier run in association with fully modelled indoor sections; some, such as Jack Ray's *Crewchester* took this to its logical conclusion by building what was effectively an indoor model railway outside in order to gain the space needed for his main concern – authentic operation of an extensive railway system.

3. Railways whose main function is to be a decorative feature of the garden. They are not required to fulfil many functions that would appeal to the more die-hard enthusiast, but are closer to being a form of garden ornament. They are usually small and simple, usually off-the-shelf, and frequently whimsical in their realisation.

Above: Detailed work permits close-ups that don't immediately show up the crudeness of semi-scale models. The stone *cei* was attempted following my visit to Laurie Wright's line, and was needed to present an attractive feature where the line passed close to the main entrance to our building, shared by owners of most of the eight apartments. In total, it is about five feet long, and nearly one foot high at its greatest. Cutting the slate on a water-fed slate cutter was a messy and noisy job, but the actual building of it was surprisingly therapeutic. The bridge is based on the cast iron one at Tan-y-bwlch, and was fretted from cold-frame acrylic sheet, with added plastic strip relief detailing.

Left: Who needs trains anyway? When you have created a scene this convincing, it provides all of the interest you need just to stand and stare... Photo: Paul Sherwood

4. Railways built for general enjoyment; they need to be reasonably sympathetic to their surroundings, but aim for a fictional recreation of general railway atmosphere; they are often their own prototypes and are frequently somewhat tongue-in-cheek. They pay a degree of attention to real railway practice, but do not wish to be constrained by it. Consequently, they normally exhibit a somewhat caricatured representation of reality, and do not obsess unduly about issues such as consistency of scale.

5. The Cinderella of the hobby seems to be the railway that sets out to be as true a representation of real railway practice as ability and circumstances will allow; collective wisdom has it that this is not really possible outdoors because of the compromises necessary to run a model railway in what is, in functional let alone scale terms, an unforgiving environment. Those that do exist are still usually freelance but they draw their rule-book directly from the real thing, employing the discipline of the parallel indoor approach. To my knowledge, there are but a few models in this country that have really developed this approach – but it is to this that can most easily be applied the term Art.

Of course we are not talking about High Art, as the necessary degree of insight may be impossible in what we do, but nonetheless, to something akin to three-dimensional painting. The purpose of Art is arguably to use the power of illusion to

Andrew Coward has also gone for expansive stations on the Isle of Westland line, even at the expense of shortening the run slightly in his restricted space. Whereas plain track can be compressed fairly easily, stations simply look unconvincing if over-shortened.

explain, communicate or express something to an audience; in as much as model-making can be a way of reflecting one's experiences of the real railway, it is performing something of the same function. The creation of high-realism indoor models is moving clearly in this direction; even the hitherto ultra-exact bible of the finescale movement, *Model Railway Journal* is increasingly recognising that a technical approach alone does not guarantee a satisfactory outcome; some artistic input is what is needed. Iain Rice has of course been arguing for many years that the best modelling is little different from a cross between painting and theatre. I see no reason why such an approach should be restricted to indoor modellers, when outdoor modelling solves many of their greatest problems at a stroke. It is this last and potentially most engaging type that the remainder of this book mainly addresses.

It is too simplistic, though, to divide something as diverse as garden railways into hard-and-fast categories; the reality is that most sit somewhere along a spectrum, and not necessarily at the same place in all respects either. (That said, achieving a degree of overall consistency has long been recognised as one of the keys to successful modelling). Some railways even have alter egos that fall in different places as well – and many suspend their disbelief in order to accommodate those fixtures of the summer, railway open days.

FORM OF ART

Nonetheless, I think it is useful to have at least a rough idea of where one falls on this scale; many factors will determine that, from personal preference to physical circumstances, technical skill and available funds. I have written this book with the last category of railway firmly in mind; this is what I personally am working towards, even though there is a long way to go fully to achieve it.

If one accepts that model making can be a minor form of art, this raises another fundamental question: for whom is it intended? This will also vary with the type of model built, though the vast majority are built solely for the satisfaction of their creator. The design implications of this are discussed in more detail later, but suffice it to point out that even if so, the artist can be his own audience, and he should therefore consider how and if he himself is likely to derive full satisfaction from his creation. Unlike indoor modelling, the exhibition circuit is not a viable proposition, so it is unlikely that mass-audiences will be an issue with a garden line, but it is equally unlikely that no one other than the builder will ever see the line; given this, to what extent should we plan to give pleasure to others with what we do?

I believe that the artistic approach need not be the exclusive domain of those with extensive gardens, and indeed my own plot is physically restrictive; constraints of size can actually work in favour of increased refinement. A decision that I took quite early on was to compensate for the small overall size of my rail-way by increasing the degree of detail and atmosphere I could realistically aim for. The best indoor models are, as with a good painting, quite simply things of beauty; for those so-inclined, the addition of Artistry has the potential to transform our models into something that is at least their equal.

I**T'S AMAZING HOW EASY IT IS** to assume that others see the world the way you do. I can't recall when I didn't have an interest in railways – even from my earliest days. One of my enduring memories is of my mother taking me to Taunton station in what must have been about 1966 or 1967 to see the trains; if only I had realised what historical gems I was probably witnessing! Model railways followed soon after, but from even that tender age, I can recall my objective as being to make the railway *realistic*. It was always planned with full scenery in mind, even if, at the age of about five, I wasn't very able to realise that plan! Ever since, from my first electric models onwards, it was always the intention to replicate the whole railway, the emphasis being on a credible location and a scene that matched what I believed that location was like – largely derived from my experiences of BR's Western Region in the mid 70s. I remember being amazed when visiting a school-friend's house, to find a railway totally devoid of scenery, but which was operated with accurate train formations and reporting numbers, so little did I suspect that others might have such a totally different slant on their experience of the same phenomenon from my own.

Through three decades of pretty constant modelling, I pursued the same objective; I have never been a particularly clubbable person, so my main inspiration was drawn from the modelling press, where the models that had the most impact were always those that were most visually convincing and which somehow possessed the strongest atmosphere.

MECHANICAL TINKERING

Hence, my eventual arrival on the garden railway scene was something of a perplexing experience. I recalled the early lines of Dave Rowlands *et al* in those *Railway Modellers* of my youth; despite the undoubted primitiveness of their models, such people excelled at conjuring up whole imagined personae for their railways, and in transmitting it through their writing. So, to find a scene apparently dominated by those whose main preoccupation seemed to be mechanical tinkering with their locomotives came as a bit of a shock. The workmanship was undoubtedly far beyond my skills, but I could not understand why many people seemed content just to run a locomotive, often on track elevated

on posts, with little in the way of railway modelling to set off their creations.

Gradually, through increasing contact with both other modellers and the folk who were volunteers on the real thing, it began to dawn on me that there are two entirely different ways of 'doing' the railway hobby. For many, the attraction is the left-brain male opportunity to tinker with machinery, oil, grease and coal, to make a machine move and do work. It is the ability to hew components from raw metal that appeals, and the pull is that of the fully equipped engineering workshop. However, this does relatively little for me; I am not especially bothered by qualifying to drive the trains, and I am much more interested in doing the customer-facing jobs. The cold machinery and materials of the metalwork shop form not my natural environment. For some, myself included, experiencing the railway is a more subjective thing – the attraction is the physical and human landscape of which the railway often became a focal point. The appeal of a red home signal is not particularly how it functions and how it is interlocked, but the visual sentry that it presents in a landscape where the rails may not even be visible – a sign that Trains Pass Here. Here one finds the aesthetic, artistic appeal of the railway – a system composed of moving metal to be sure, but also one that exists in a specific place and time, that does a specific job, and serves or employs specific people. The excitement of the steam engine comes not purely from its mechanical functioning but the mysterious emotional impact that this most living of inanimate machines seems to exert even on generations who have no memories of the 'golden age' of steam.

RECREATING ONE'S EXPERIENCE

I am, of course, exaggerating the divide: in fact, the two approaches are opposite sides of the same coin. Even the most hardened engineer must find his fundamental motivation from some kind of subjective passion for what he is doing, and even the most subjective viewer like me cannot help but be intrigued by the functioning of such a complex system and those various aesthetic experiences that accompany it. But it nonetheless seems to me that there are two quite distinct camps when it comes to railway enthusiasts, and in as much as modelling is a

Railway hardware: for many, the attraction is purely the trains, but in this classic scene from the Ffestiniog Railway, it is the context of the scene that really sets off those fine double Fairlies to their best. The tight curvature of the tracks leads the eye to the subject, and allows the train to be seen behind the locomotive. While our railways are clearly much more than mere photo-sets, the compositional techniques of the photographer can be useful in devising scenes that will enhance our experience of the machinery, too. Notice also, the relative size of the trains and the buildings behind them; in model form, this would be very useful for screening out unwanted background clutter.

Above: This is what it is all about for me – a live steam train in a landscape that is so 'true' that it could be real. My newly lined Russell takes a train down the line on the inspirational Tarren Hendre Railway. Photo: Gavin Robertshaw

Right: Bill Winter's line is an interesting case. Bill insists that he is purely a 'hardware' man, and that design in the sense discussed here didn't come into it. However, he concedes that a lifetime of watching railways has probably influenced what he builds, and he has created this superbly atmospheric line at his home on Anglesey. Bill works at 22.5mm:1ft, in other words, 2ft gauge on 45mm gauge track. Whatever his motivations, just notice the well-observed detail Bill has included, such as that gate across the track, complete with bolt detail on the strapping, and the superb rolling stock in the background. An example of art and engineering coming together if ever there was one. Photo: David Halfpenny

Left: Paul Sherwood's Maesffordd & Nant Gorris Railway was one of the first 'realistic' garden models I visited. Luckily, Paul lives little more than an hour's drive away, and many a pleasant afternoon has been spent running on his line. Here we see Nant Gorris Station, clearly inspired by those on the Corris and Talyllyn lines; again, good composition and natural materials create a real sense of place and authenticity. Photo: Sara Stock

Lower: More artistry on Tarren Hendre. The view down this ravine from the quarry has been wonderfully contrived by Jeremy Ledger, and is another example of those intriguing little corners that one can incorporate, to be discovered by the determined explorer. Of course, this sort of work really needs to be designed at the initial construction stage; we are talking here as much about garden design as model railways. Photo: Andrew Crookell

he who is primarily interested in building and running a model locomotive, he for whom the functioning of the machinery was perhaps more important than its appearance, let alone its historical authenticity. For such people the mere existence of a track on which to run their models was sufficient. So long as it did not upset the domestic authorities (too much) it did not matter if it didn't look very pretty; it was more important to have the track positioned at a convenient operating height than at one which integrated it into the garden, and given that the models were manually controlled, a key objective was to minimise any negative impact of the topography on the permanent way. In some instances, shrubs were planted to reduce the frankly grotesque impact that such structures could have on the average garden, but in terms of 'scenery' that was often about it.

MODEL RAILWAY PRACTICE

And such have garden railways in the wider sense mostly remained ever since. The august body of persons known as the Gauge 1 Model Railway Association still largely adheres to these established principles, though even there, things seem to be changing slowly as younger people join the fold. Narrow Gauge modellers on the other hand, have tended to develop a somewhat wider take on their activities, though ancillary railway equipment has still remained largely subsidiary to the activity of running the trains. In the meantime, indoor models have seen levels of commercial and technological growth that are light years ahead of the garden scales, and the *avant guard* of the modelling community has pressed the frontiers to the point that on occasions it can be impossible to distinguish between a photo of a model and one of the real thing. It is my guess that many among the established generation of garden modellers are quite happy with this state of affairs, given that their field has come to be seen as the refuge of those deterred by the mass commercialisation of the indoor scene.

However, to me, coming to garden railways as an aspirational fine-scale modeller, it was easy to be dismayed. Many functions of what I took to be normal model railway practice were simply absent, such as realistic track layouts, purposeful operating and convincing-looking infrastructure. In many ways, garden railways seemed to be where indoor modelling had been several decades previously. Overriding all appeared to be the rationale

means of expressing or recreating one's experience, the two groups seem inclined to produce quite different kinds of model, be they indoors or out.

Within the spectrum of 'reduced size' railways, garden railways occupy a unique and rather uncomfortable position: anything much larger becomes the realm of the ride-on machinery of the true model engineer; anything smaller is clearly the domain of the modeller, since the techniques and materials in use are unlikely to excite those who get their kicks from lengths of mild steel. Garden railways of the size we are primarily interested in here, within the scale bracket roughly 1:12 to 1:20 of full size reasonably attract interest from both camps. That said, it seems to me that the model engineers still generally hold sway. This is not surprising since until recently, it has been necessary to manufacture quite a lot of the hardware oneself, and there is no escaping the fact that that requires hardware-type skills.

Since garden railways go back further than indoor models, the tradition of garden railways has been that of the engineer,

Above: How the would-be artist suffers for his craft! The total population of Castle Bryan seen looking guiltily through the station roof...
A perpetual challenge is to build structures that not only look delicate, but are also still sufficiently strong for the rigours of outdoor life.

Centre: Artistry doesn't have to be confined to trains... Photo: Sara Stock

Top right: For me, a garden railway is about far more than the days when trains run. This shot was taken when I had gone out to refill our birdfeeder. For only a few minutes, the sun caught the station building at QFR, and I was just in time to grab my camera to record this tranquil moment.

Lower right: Bill Winter's line does have a significant difficulty in the form of the chain-link fence at the edge of his property, an issue yet to be fully resolved – but don't let that detract from your appreciation of that superbly railway-like scene in front. Photo: David Halfpenny

that the outdoors is a place that enforces severe restrictions on what modelling is practically possible. Into this camp fell the notion that fine detail is not feasible because it is too easily damaged, and not necessary because it cannot, in any case, be seen. It also dictated that, at all costs, one should build a level line to minimise the effects of gradients on the running and controllability of the models. Furthermore, it appeared to say that if you have no space for a continuous run, you should give up there and then.

A Wooden Baseboard

When you are new to something, it is the easiest thing in the world just to go along with the way it appears always to have been done. I went out and bought a couple of the then-new Accucraft Lynton & Barnstaple wagons – fine models so far as they go, and they did at least allow me to adjust my mental image of the size of 16mm models to something closer to the reality. My first attempts at making buildings and rolling stock were quite crude, not because I was incapable of making them otherwise, but simply because that was what accepted thinking seemed to imply one should do, and it was all I had at that time seen while visiting a few other railways.

However, as a relatively experienced modeller, the learning curve was travelled quite rapidly. I began to appreciate at first hand the peculiar brand of magic that garden railways can exert. For all the compromise, they possess a potential that no indoor modeller has available, in that they exist in the real world in their own right, rather than in the sterile parallel universe of a wooden baseboard. They have an uncanny ability to dissolve the gross conflicts of scale and proportion that exist between modelled world and its full-size surroundings – and they are large enough to be considered to be railways in their own right.

Many more of the concerns of running a real railway apply to a garden line, simply because of its location, while its size means that material and mechanical functionality also reflects more closely that of the full size thing. I began to see why some garden modellers don't feel the need for anything more than a representation of a railway.

Irish-Inspired Line

Nonetheless, my own thinking started to head clearly down another path, and this was encouraged by encounters with the work of those few who were also striving to do something different. Neil Ramsay's exquisite hand-built rolling stock was clear proof that it is perfectly possible to run finely detailed models in the outdoors. The fine visual effect of his Irish-inspired line was much closer to what I was looking for. The chance discovery online of Paul Sherwood's Maesfordd & Nant Gorris railway, built scarcely an hour's drive from my home, and my subsequent visits, drove the determination further, and this was later reinforced by seeing what has to be one of the most impressive garden railways ever built in the U.K., Jeremy Ledger's Tarren Hendre. Here, at last, was demonstrable proof that something equating to fine-scale modelling is possible out of doors and on an ambitious scale at that.

In 2006, Paul Sherwood and I founded an email group to try to pull those few people together in to a forum dedicated to discussing this more holistic approach to garden railways, and to our surprise it flourished and grew to include over two hundred and fifty members around the world – small fry against the thousands in the wider hobby, but sufficient to encourage us all to persevere in the knowledge that it is far from an impossible task to take an artistic rather than an engineering approach to railways in the garden. The question we are all working on is – How?

IMAGINE STANDING ON THE CREST OF A HILL on a summer's after-noon; below you is laid out the broad sweep of the North Wales countryside, the straight, deep valley leading down to the silver glint of the *traeth* or estuary in the distance; the undulations of the Trawsfynedd plateau stretching into the distance. Below you, a small railway line skirts the hillside, often on stone embankments, piercing a ridge, then disappearing through some trees and re-emerging to cross itself, and disappear once more uphill into the gnarled old trees of the remnant Welsh forest. A hint of smoke down the valley awakens your hopes; ears straining, you start to make out the sound of a narrow-gauge engine working hard. Its whistle affirms more distinctly its existence. But it is still mostly out of sight. Several minutes pass, the sound growing louder, until the train swings into view, clinging to the hillside, the coaches snaking closely behind. The double blast from the twin chimneys of the Fairlie passes below you, before the train swings hard right, flanges squealing on the curve – then almost silence. But almost immediately, the twin smoke columns again betray the train's position, before it re-emerges on the upper part of the line, head-on towards you, locomotive power-bogie waggling slightly under the load and gradient, sweeping over the line it has just traversed, and on up into the trees, the familiar sound of wheel on rail following behind, the trail of smoke tracing the train's progress until it disappears...

No prizes for guessing the location on the Festiniog Railway – or the clichéd evocation, but most of us have been there – or somewhere equally evocative, sometime. For me, creating a garden railway is about trying to capture the essence of this or similar experiences in my own garden, so that I can live them time and time again...

FROM GREAT STRENGTH CAME FORTH SWEETNESS...

Some years ago, I paid a visit to the Welsh Highland Railway in Porthmadog; I was in search of the legendary *Russell*, long one of my favourite narrow gauge locomotives. Unfortunately,

what I found was a pile of components liberally scattered around the workshops and yard – *Russell* was in the middle of a major restoration project.

What struck me forcefully was the way in which a steam locomotive is more than just the sum of its parts. The pair of side tanks that were the most identifiable parts of the locomotive visible were just a couple of uninteresting metal boxes resting on a wagon. Yet when assembled into a locomotive, such parts become something more than mere metal boxes – they somehow become part of something living...

The same could be said for the railway as a whole: take a series of wooden posts, a pile of stones, and some oddly shaped bits of metal. Assemble them in a particular way, and add various mechanical linkages and probably some masonry structures; an alien would still be hard-pressed to work out what it was all for. And yet, as we know, this peculiar agglomeration of components is capable of something more; thus does a set of cold, engineering components become the familiar thing that captivates so many people. What we are talking about again, is the Art of Railways.

I defy anyone who has a passion for railways to escape it; for even those whose drug of choice is pure steel, I suspect that it is the subjective response to the mechanics of the railway that is really what enthuses – the way in which those lengths of steel can be made to do work, the way in which they can be made to move with a certain poetry. After all, we are human, and we see the world in subjective, not objective terms. While the engineering drawing can communicate the technicalities, it takes a painting, photograph or personal memory to express what those components become when assembled to make a railway.

LOCOMOTIVE WORKING HARD

What the engineering drawings *cannot* show is the drama that accompanies the whole. The passing of a train appeals to people because it is a piece of theatre; even the very linear shape of a train implies movement and direction, the way in which it is prefaced by changing signals, the way it appears, approaches, passes and disappears from view appeals to so many people – not just railway enthusiasts – exactly because it is a drama; the sight of a locomotive working hard, and the associated sequence of sounds merely enhancing the experience. What is more, this drama takes place within the outdoor world, where the sensory elements of our relationship with nature can enhance it, and it also encompasses a multitude of human stories, whether of the locomotive crew, the station staff, the traveller, or even just the onlooker.

And the lesson for the garden modeller? The mechanics may be intriguing, but if you want to recreate the experience of the real railway, you need to pay attention to the subjective as well as the objective aspects. After all, in our gardens, we have at our disposal so many of the elements that make the real thing what it is.

For various reasons, garden narrow gauge has seemed especially concerned with the mechanics of the railway; most effort goes into making things work. While that left-brain activity of Tinkering is undoubtedly necessary to construct a model railway of any sort, garden NG uniquely seems less concerned with how the finished mechanisms look. I have lost count of the number of ingenious 'bodgelled' contraptions that I have seen wheezing their way around one line or another. While they (mostly) work on a mechanical level, and some are indeed intriguing, few

Opposite: Andrew Coward has used the theatrical screening potential of vegetation on his Isle of Westland line. His locomotives almost have to force their way between the trees, building a tremendous sense of anticipation as they approach…

Above: Trains enter stage left over Glen Olibhe Viaduct, although at present this remains in a fairly rudimentary form. The bridge has been built with the express intention of amplifying track noise in order to attract the attention. The secret seems to be in fixing the track down hard so that noise is transmitted to the bridge deck.

Right: A quiet moment at Nant Gorris. Paul Sherwood has included sufficient detail in his cameos to create life and believability, but not so much that the simple tranquillity of the scene is overwhelmed. Notice too, the restrained use of colour in Paul's palette.

bear anything more than a passing resemblance to any piece real railway that I have ever seen. In pure tinkering terms, they probably hit the mark, but for my money, railway modelling they are not.

The Gauge 1 fraternity can hardly be accused of majoring on the 'soft' elements of railways – theirs is largely the stuff of fully-fledged, red-blooded model engineers. Yet their norm is to go to great lengths to make their models not only function well, but to look like exquisite reproductions of the real thing. They accept that to hit all the buttons, you have to attend to the *visual* as well as the engineering appeal, even if they are often less interested in doing so beyond just the trains. And indeed, the great railway engineers of the past knew the same – considerable effort was put by almost all into making their locomotives (and indeed the rest of their railway systems) things of *beauty* as well as power.

ART OF RAILWAYS

From an enthusiasts' perspective, it is the Art of Railways that comes less easily. Perhaps it really does come down to the way in which our (male) brains are wired: how many thousands of three-quarter view railway photographs are taken for each individual more striking, artistically arranged one? And how many predictable, formulaic models are built for each really inspiring one? Perhaps it really doesn't matter so long as those individuals are happy, but for me at least, seeking a rather more unconventional inspiration, it seems like so many wasted opportunities. And you only have to see the crowds round the really inspiring bits of railway – be they real or model – to see that I am not alone.

In the garden, we have a head start on our indoor colleagues; their blank baseboard is exactly that, no more, no less. On top of that same baseboard can go exactly what the builder chooses – the most basic train set, or the most exquisite piece of crafts-manship. While that may be an opportunity, it also presents the builder with sole responsibility for the outcome: every last aspect of the model will have to be contrived from nothing. In the garden, things are different. We already have large elements of our final model in place: the lighting has already been sorted for us, as has the basic terrain. Weathering will be provided free of charge and our vegetation will develop for itself so long as we don't actually kill it in the meantime. The materials at our disposal are mostly the 'real thing'. And yet, by convention, most effort goes into building a garden railway in *spite* of those inherent advantages, of overcoming the problems they pose, rather than exploiting the opportunities they offer. The artistry of the situation is thereby killed, and with it, I would argue, is any real appeal of the outcome; by focusing on a narrow part of the railway experience, we risk omitting much of what makes the railway appealing in the first place. Just as with real railway engineers, of course we need to pay attention to the functioning of the individual bits of wood and metal, but just as with the real railway, we need to ensure that they come together in such a way that our railways, too, become more

Above: The play in progress. The village Open Gardens weekend, with a healthy number of spectators enjoying the increased spectacle of Stage 3. It is traditional to perform the Lower Bryandale One-Step when trains cross the viaduct. Photo: Sara Stock

Lower: It is possible, these days, to achieve very realistic results when modelling in the indoor scales. This is my 'diversion' for the dark, wet nights of winter when a little therapy rather than construction is required. The baseboard offers the possibility to shape the model almost limitlessly, and I have tried to use some of those theatrical techniques to create a pleasing scene in a very small area (about 7ft x 15in) – but it still somehow lacks the *life* of the garden railway. Conventionally, garden railways have been thought of as being far more restricted in terms of realism than indoor models, but I am not so sure.

Above: Tunnels, of course, have huge theatrical potential, whether for trains entering or leaving them – a situation made all the better by the exhaust that our locomotives put out; bridges can also capitalise somewhat on the effect of steam hitting the underside of the arch. While tunnels have major implications for practicality, it is surely worth building them properly, with a lined interior (so that the exhaust lingers and leaks out most effectively) and as dark as possible; Laurie Wright has managed this admirably. The effect of a tail lamp receding into the darkness is worth the effort...

Top right: The dark, dank places on a railway also have a strong sense of drama. This cutting on Tarren Hendre is a classic of the genre, and while this view is only available to the camera, it still looks the part even from usual viewing distances.

Right: This view is also rather bare at present, but it will one day form the climax of the climb up from Minffordd, with trains bursting from the trees onto the viaduct, before rounding the ledge and disappearing up the line.

than just the sum of their parts. From the mechanical strength of the railway, we need to draw forth the artistic sweetness needed to charm one and all.

DEPTH OF FIELD

A lot has been written by the likes of Iain Rice about methods of presentation for indoor model railways. He was thinking especially about exhibition layouts, where one is considering how people other than oneself experience one's work. He came to the conclusion that there are many similarities between exhibiting a model railway and experiencing a play at a theatre. Just as at a theatre, where you would not expect to be able to see backstage (though you would also expect the sight lines to be suitable for comfortable viewing), then the same should

apply to a model. In a theatre, the set designer might manipulate these same issues to control what the audience sees, and also to make certain dramatic effects possible. In a theatre, just as on a railway, a set of mundane components is made to take on a different life under certain controlled circumstances.

In their final development, Rice's ideas took the form of a full-scale proscenium with concealed lighting and 'wings', into which trains went 'off-stage'. He raised the viewing height until most viewers were looking across to the layout rather than down on it, and he took great care to ensure that 'entries' end 'exits' were masked with the equivalent of stage flats. He went further to suggest that the entire scene should be assembled in the way that an artist or photographer would attempt to do, considering issues such as symmetry, visual composition and balance, and possibly depth of field. He considered the impact of

An intending passenger's eye view of the trains. Using view-blockers to part-conceal views is one of the most effective visual teases in the business. You can suggest almost limitless possibilities and have people craning their necks (metaphorically at least) to know what is just round the corner. The same effect can be achieved by making things, such as railway track, apparently disappear to the vanishing point.
Photo: Sara Stock

various lighting effects on the experience. Having seen a number of layouts that adopted these principles, there is no doubt in my mind that the experience of the viewer is significantly enhanced as a result, while the models themselves are set off to their best advantage.

How much of Rice's thinking is relevant for garden railways? Well, perhaps it partly depends on whom you consider you are building the model 'for'. One of the enduring stereotypes of eccentrics who do mad things like building garden railways is of some one who is away with the fairies, totally wrapped up in their own little make-believe world. We all know that isn't true, don't we? However, if you are solely concerned with your own experience of your model, maybe it is not really very important what the thing looks like; your imagination will be telling you more than enough stories to cover for any aesthetic deficiencies in what you are doing. But there are, in reality, few people who have the luxury of being 'railway hermits'. By far the largest number of railways by necessity occupy the only bit of land most of us are ever likely to own – the back garden. While this means that they are neatly tucked away from general public gaze, there is still the fact that the garden will probably be required to perform other functions too, and at very least, not be a complete eyesore next to our homes. Other members of the family, and visitors (whether railway-orientated or not) will inevitably gaze out over our empires, and should we hold an open day, the most discerning audience of all will be coming to call… And I would argue that even with a 'sole-viewer' model, it is worth the effort of setting off our work in an attractive way – there can be few times where it will not enhance our own experience – and after all, aren't we worth it?

Gaining permission from the domestic authorities to build the line in the first place may well be dependent on its final appearance and its impact on other users of the garden. In my own case, the critical reaction of those nearest to what I have been doing has been instructive and useful in itself.

Wider Visual Impact

The converted Victorian school, of which we occupy a large part of the ground floor, contains eight apartments. We were fortunate collectively to be able to buy the freehold at an early stage, so we are in effect our own landlords; had this not been the case,

the LBR would probably never have got off the drawing board in the first place. What is more, the only piece of available land is at the side and front of the property, so there was no way this railway was going to be out of sight – and just to complicate matters, the building is also situated in a conservation area within a small, historic town. This did not create any statutory restrictions, but I felt bound to bear in mind the wider visual impact of my activities on a street that contains many attractive gardens and which receives a significant number of visitors in summer. All this meant that I had to consider to a much greater degree, the impact of what I was building not only on my own family but also on my neighbours.

In the early stages, the line was tucked away up the side of the building, outside our own windows and hemmed in by a tall privet hedge belonging to the adjacent property. The space is barely six feet wide, and so the railway was all but invisible – apart from the section on the front of the building where the site widened, the only space sufficient to consider a one hundred and eighty-plus degree return curve. For many months even the other residents remained ignorant of the railway, and it only became apparent at the stage where I constructed the return curve on a viaduct. I was not quite sure what would be the reaction of passers-by; if anything, I expected some smirking and leg pulling. What I ended up with was a local attraction that stopped many people of all ages in their tracks, and which quite overwhelmed me with their interest and enthusiasm for what I had built.

There is no longer any doubt in *my* mind that not only is it possible to disarm the condescension of non-believers, but that garden railways can actually be a positive focal point for one's garden, friends and family. Vandalism is (touch wood) not an issue here; regrettably that probably is not so for large parts of our country – though I do wonder whether the defensive approach of looking menacingly at anyone who dares to approach perhaps invites more trouble than a more relaxed but confident one.

Running the Trains

When it came to Phase Three, I really expected that my neighbours who had so far tolerated my eccentricities, would object to having the railway continuing right across the front of the building in which they would one day need to try to sell their property. We undertook the extension as part of a necessary remodelling of that part of the garden, and said that it would only go ahead with unanimous agreement. What I did not expect was the enthusiastic encouragement which was their actual response. So, Phase Three went ahead in early 2008, but this time with a much more conscious effort to create something that would appeal to my, by now, regular public. While topography and previous alignments dictated quite a lot, I tried to plan the extension mindful of the idea of a stage setting, with a clear composition when seen from the public side in terms of planting, topography and scene setting.

So, to return to my initial question: to what extent does a garden railway need to be 'staged'? Since few lines are seen by no one other than their creator, and to the extent that you can also consider yourself to be your own audience, I would argue

Bridge and ledge at top of gradient – climax of the drama as trains burst out from behind the plants, working hard. Effect enhanced by limiting length of cameo; Trains exit by curving out of view.

Station and passing loop in front of viewer – secondary focal point of 'picture'

Viaduct by which trains enter stage right (with noise effect on bridge).

Alternatively, a Gradient presents backdrop – as at Beddgelert – will be mostly hidden behind planting in due course. Planting will also provide a green backdrop for the station and hide building wall.

Station building in front of platform; view blocker, and also gives on-lookers the would-be passenger's perspective. This and the future signal adjacent to it will eventually be lit to add life at dusk – should appeal to passers-by!

Siding adds operational interest, and also a place to display stock. Can also accommodate a banker for heavy trains.

From the path to the front door (out of shot to the left), this wall and bridge present an attractive prospect. Good spot for low-level photo's or inspection of models, too.

that this notion is very relevant to the garden scene – but it is one that seems often forgotten when we become pre-occupied with solving the practical, constructional difficulties that our plans can present. Any other planned form of garden is, after all, a highly staged affair, the manipulation of natural features to achieve a desired aesthetic effect; not only may such an approach assist in winning approval from the necessary domestic authorities but the whole experience of running the trains will be enhanced by a line where careful thought has been given to choreographing what happens. Try thinking of your activity, for a moment, not as a type of railway modelling, but as a type of gardening…

As with a stage, there are a number of issues that need consideration: the general composition and balance of the set, the opportunities for the actors to enter and leave, and the ways in which they will move around whilst on stage. Unlike most stages, however, we normally view our gardens from multiple viewpoints: what we are dealing with is something more akin to theatre in the round. We need to bear in mind the ways in which trains appear when they are moving, and the subjective responses that this can engender – the effect of a train gradually coming towards you down

The Tarren Hendre Railway is a line with a strong vertical component; the tallest landscape features are between five and six feet tall. The mature planting accentuates this further.

This vista makes excellent use of the tree trunks of the existing planting to frame the view.

In a garden of this size, the hard landscaping can be ambitious – rock based terrain provides a defining line to the back of the model, behind which general vegetation softens the effect.

Even the bridges maintain the visual theme. The upper one provides for an intriguing glimpse of a distant train when one passes over.

New, railway related planting capitalises on the verticals too, in the chose of plants.

a long straight can build anticipation, while the effect of one moving round a curve can be quite different, especially if viewed end-on, with the head and the tail of the train momentarily moving in opposing directions, the train itself flexing gracefully as it rounds the curve. Making trains work hard uphill towards a summit can also create a very successful dramatic climax, while their intimate passage, merely glimpsed, through dense undergrowth is the equivalent of theatrical suspense.

LEVEL CROSSING GATES

Anticipation is a major part of many railway experiences: the presence of shiny rails is the only clue one needs to understand instantly that this is a place where trains pass; they will appear from and disappear to predictable locations – what is unknown is the time scale. If you happen to be positioned where you can hear the bell codes in a nearby signal box, see the closing of level crossing gates, or a semaphore signal nodding its approving head, these only heighten the anticipation of what is about to happen. Trains possess superb dramatic timing – the intervals between them is normally neither too short nor too long, and their arrival is often prefaced in a way unmatched by any other form of transport. Even on the modern high-tech railway, the drama is still there, as a speeding express disappears from view, the multiple aspect colour lights shifting down their sequence behind it, dust and litter kicked up in a temporary storm through which you can make out that flashing tail-light. Times may have changed, but much of the magic hasn't!

The kind of rural, low-key activity that we mostly try to recreate on NG garden lines is rather different, but there is still plenty to harness in terms of adding 'theatre' to our experience. Key to this is interrupting the view of the trains so that we are effectively creating the same opportunities for them to enter and exit the stage as on the real thing. Maybe it is more a matter of pushing through the undergrowth, Talyllyn-style than tearing down a main line, but the intent is the same, and the best opportunity for doing this is when planning the trajectory of the line. Anticipating key sightlines is important here, though not always an easy feat given the time that planting will take to mature before the final effect is achieved. To some extent, the planting itself can be used to manipulate the view available, and indeed to mask undesired features.

Andrew Coward has made superb use of this device on his Isle of Westland line in Kent. His garden is small, and the track plan a folded figure-of-eight, with two loops effectively running more or less parallel to each other round much of the garden. Andrew has used subtle differences of height and a screen of plants between the two loops to focus the view on the desired area, while masking completely the 'unreal' parallel track issue.

TAIL LAMP AGLOW

We can also use those other qualities that our trains possess, which are lacking on indoor models, namely sound and steam. Another way of building the anticipation for a passing train is to enhance the way in which it approaches, deliberately playing with the various senses. If it can be arranged that the train can be heard before it can be seen, then perhaps its steam and where fitted, its lights appear before the full thing becomes visible, the arrival on-stage of the star becomes the climax of a drama rather than just yet another circuit of the lawn perimeter. On my LBR, I have deliberately deployed such tricks in full public gaze: the main passing station sits right at the front of the plot under the viewers' noses – an ideal place for a train to wait, gently hissing, for 'something else' to happen – and given that the pavement is about two and a half feet below the garden, at a good viewing height too. In either direction, the line climbs steeply away, in one direction describing a 180° curve in about

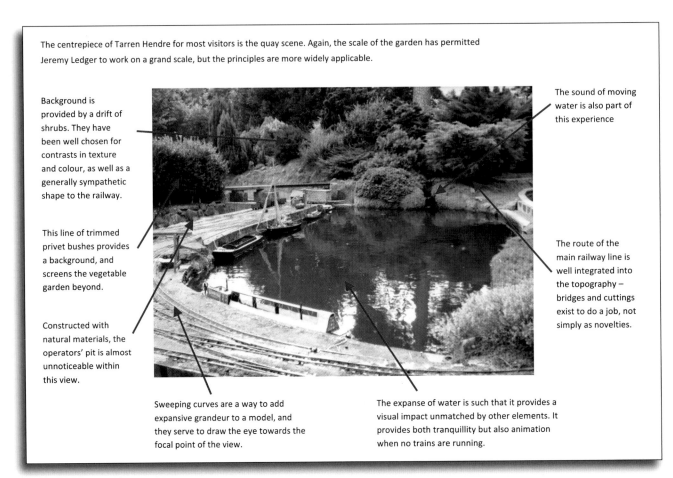

The centrepiece of Tarren Hendre for most visitors is the quay scene. Again, the scale of the garden has permitted Jeremy Ledger to work on a grand scale, but the principles are more widely applicable.

Background is provided by a drift of shrubs. They have been well chosen for contrasts in texture and colour, as well as a generally sympathetic shape to the railway.

This line of trimmed privet bushes provides a background, and screens the vegetable garden beyond.

Constructed with natural materials, the operators' pit is almost unnoticeable within this view.

The sound of moving water is also part of this experience

The route of the main railway line is well integrated into the topography – bridges and cuttings exist to do a job, not simply as novelties.

Sweeping curves are a way to add expansive grandeur to a model, and they serve to draw the eye towards the focal point of the view.

The expanse of water is such that it provides a visual impact unmatched by other elements. It provides both tranquillity but also animation when no trains are running.

An unexpected effect of building the line so close to the house was that each window effectively presents a framed view of the line, and one can work one's way round the house, effectively seeing a picture-guide to the top half of the line. This is the view from one of the two bedroom windows, and might explain why the LBR has come to be such an integral part of the day-to-day life of our home.

eight feet of width, climbing over a stone embankment and bridge, and then meandering back across the plot on a 1:35 gradient. In the fullness of time, much of the climb will be hidden by planting, with viewers gaining just glimpses of trains dropping down the line before emerging from the plants, and rounding the curve into the station. Beddgelert on the Welsh Highland Railway with its reverse curves on the hillside above was great inspiration. Travelling in the other direction, the run will hopefully be more dramatic still, with trains curving out of the station, disappearing into the 'trees', before bursting out again some twenty feet further on, nearly a foot higher, crossing a metre-wide bridge and rounding a rocky ledge before disappearing up the line, tail lamp aglow. All it will take is a couple of years for the plants to mature…

It does not, however, require such dramatics to achieve a similar effect. By definition, such a scene is probably the focal point of a railway, and too many such locations would both be self-defeating and rather overwhelming; every symphony needs its slow movement too. We can nonetheless use the same notion of staging for smaller, less showy stretches of track. Large-scale models gift us another advantage here: the human field of vision does not change as we shift the scale of our modelling. Conventional wisdom suggests that about six feet away, our lateral field of vision is not more than four to six feet. In that distance can be contained an entire N gauge model railway, but in the garden scales, it represents nothing more than a small cameo. Given suitable 'view framers' our trains will pass naturally into, across and out of our field of vision in a way that small scale models do not. Within the space so contained, we have the possibility of creating a cameo scene to give even a small section a focal point. Again, this can be over-done; not every space needs to be action packed, and that focal point need be nothing more than, say, a PW hut, a line side sign or some milk churns. While on this subject, a useful tip I learned

from my local florist is to arrange such items in odd numbers: every florist knows, she said, that even numbers of things instantly look contrived, and having tried it, I agree.

THE OVERALL EFFECT

A slightly more ambitious application of the same effect can be achieved by blocking part of the middle of a cameo by positioning, say, a plant or a building in front of the line. Almost every station I have ever seen on a garden railway placed the track at the front and the platform and buildings at the back. While there are clearly certain practicalities to consider, such as access to the trains, points etc., not only does this become very predictable, but it also means that the viewer sees the station from a different viewpoint from that of an intending passenger. Simply turning the thing around and placing the platform and buildings between the trains and the viewer can achieve a completely different effect. This gives a more concealed but more intriguing view; the loss of sight of the platform elevation of the building is more than offset, and in some plans one may also gain in practical terms from bringing any sidings towards to front of the scene where they are both more easily reached, and parked wagons can more easily add to the overall effect.

A final consideration is how the line looks when no trains are running. In my quest for realism, I believe it is essential for the entire infrastructure to be in position permanently. If buildings and so on are removed between running sessions, the entire character of the railway as a permanent feature in its own right is completely destroyed. I believe that a garden railway should exist in its full form constantly, even if that does have implications for construction techniques and maintenance of buildings and the like. What is more important is that the line looks as if a train *could* pass at any moment, even when we know one won't. After all, real NG lines spent most of their life in a state of suspended animation, with trains only occasionally raising the dust. Other props can support this illusion: the signal standing set at danger; an old wagon gently rusting at the end of a siding, the locomotive shed with its doors locked shut – who knows if there is steam being raised just behind them? In actual fact, like many I know, I don't actually need to *run* trains at all – it can be all one needs to gaze out of the window on a fine evening at that track snaking away into the bushes…

CHAPTER five

NARROW GAUGE LINES always have been the mavericks of the railway world – the place where the normal rules didn't apply. They come in all shapes and sizes, from tiny mineral lines such as those that served industries in, amongst other places Northamptonshire and Dorset, to networks that were for all intents and purposes main lines that just happened to run on narrower than usual tracks – into that category, I suppose, fell the Lynton and Barnstaple and even the Ffestiniog. And if you look beyond the UK, you can still find systems that operate in such a way, the modern metre gauge network of Switzerland being a notable example. Going back in time somewhat, one can think of such impressive systems as those of South Africa with its NG16 Garratt locomotives. So narrow gauge in a purely literal sense of the word is really a licence to do just about anything, but despite that, the term has come to mean something more figurative – a particular *genus* of railway, self-contained, eccentric, normally decrepit and definitely whimsical – and I think it is fair to say that the larger NG networks managed to perpetuate some of these characteristics even when they effectively became the standard gauge of the areas they served. Perhaps it all comes down to that slightly crazy, top-heavy impression that NG machinery gives courtesy of that small distance between the rails.

FREELANCE MODELLER

It is interesting to note just how many garden railway modellers are involved with one or other of the preserved NG railways in the UK, far more in percentage terms, I would estimate, than could be said for those who model in the smaller scales. I wonder whether this betrays our true orientation! Yet despite this, the prototype is something that garden modellers seem to have an arm's length relationship with when it comes to their own creations. Part of this perhaps stems from that determinedly independent streak that insists that the garden line is not a model at all, instead simply a very small but very real railway in its own right. If this is so, then it needs to have no prototype except itself. This is a very convenient 'get-out' clause for those who love to tinker with all manner of mechanical contraptions, since authenticity simply does not enter into it; the maker can be complete master of his creation – and who would gainsay that? However, there are very few lines which do not purport to work to some kind of at least fairly consistent scale, and that in turn is implicit acceptance that the garden railway has some kind of relationship with something that is a larger version of itself. The readily

available track systems come in few gauges, and that dictates to some extent the scale of everything else – even the most determined freelance modeller will probably adopt something that equates roughly to about 18, 24 or 36in gauge. Beyond that, the imagination is the limit.

One can speculate over the extent to which this approach derived from a genuine desire to be a complete free spirit, or simply the technical difficulties of building fully functioning models, often steam powered, and sturdy enough for garden use. The original Archangel 'Brick' may have turned out to be a seminal locomotive in the history of garden railway development, but it was never going to win any prizes for prototype fidelity. Contrast that with the latest products, some thirty years later, from the likes of Roundhouse and Accucraft, which are increasingly converging with their indoor cousins in terms of detailing and reliability, even if there is still some way to go before we achieve a truly fine scale live steam ready-to-run model; is it significant that those companies have noticed a growing demand for accurate scale models of prototypes rather than the semi-scale generic locomotives hitherto produced – or are they actually driving the process? Perhaps it simply reflects the fact that the incoming generation of garden modellers is more likely to have come up through the ranks of indoor modellers and less likely to be a down-sizing model engineer than used to be the case. Either way, the purchase of a (reasonably) scale model of a prototype marks a significant transition: the acceptance that one is at least in part trying to replicate something that ran on a 'real' railway in the full-size world. This does not mean that one then has to go flat-out to create a prototypical model railway – even indoors, probably the most common scenario is the historical 'might-have-been', where elements of prototype practice are blended into a more or less plausible fictional setting, and there is no reason why we should not do the same. Many NG locomotives were either production runs, or shared design and components with similar locomotives elsewhere; many Hunslets, for example, shared a certain house-style. Thus one's locomotive can easily be considered to be another of the same 'class' as its more famous inspiration – and if you want a different livery from the original, then why not?

PROTOTYPICAL FIDELITY

A further step is to aim to create models of the original locomotives, but then consider them to be running on a different railway. In the preservation period, locomotive swaps are far from unusual, and even in early times, locomotive such as the classic *Russell* ran in numerous parts of the country during its life. A similar gradation of study can be applied to rolling stock and ancillary structures such as buildings. The degree to which you personally take this approach is clearly a matter of individual preference, but I have found that with increasing experience, I am moving further down the prototypical fidelity approach.

I had one of those 'magic moments' in spring 2008, when the roof finally went on to the Curly Roofed Van. All of a sudden, the thing gained the character of the original – that roofline that I had been staring at on photographs and drawings for months previously was suddenly there in three-dimensional form in front of me. It was essential for the character of the vehicle that the subtle curves were captured just so, and fortunately a good set of drawings ensured that this did actually happen.

There is no substitute for visiting the real thing in terms of
inspiration derived. Even in their rather sanitised preserved
forms, the 'heritage' railways do exude character and give
a quite good sense of how the original must have looked –
albeit with the grime and neglect stripped away. I took this
picture of Rhydoronen on the Talyllyn line in spring 2008,
but it could almost be any time in the last century or so.

Left: The original 1873 station building at Tan-y-bwlch was another 'must model' item, so I took the opportunity to photograph it on a visit in early 2008. Apart from its general attractiveness, it struck me as a suitably small building to model at full scale on a restricted site. The wooden construction was also a welcome relief from the as-yet unresolved issue of fully convincing stone modelling. However, three-quarter views such as this are of less use than the following picture for scaling drawings from – which is an essential step in capturing the character of the original, especially when you don't have the original drawings.

Lower: Square-on elevation shots are much more helpful from a technical modelling point of view. Even better is to incorporate a known dimension, such as a ranging rod into the picture.

Some indoor modellers have it that nothing is more convincing than a model of a true prototype, and I can increasingly see where they are coming from; what is more, fact can often turn out to be stranger than fiction – but even here, such eccentricity looks to my eye most convincing when it has been derived from real life.

For me, this responds to my objective of using my modelling as a vehicle for further understanding of prototype practice, and the researching of a project prior to commencing the actual building has become in itself a more and more absorbing exercise. When you have modelled in detail a real artefact, you feel that you have gained a greater understanding of its design, appearance and function, and there is something magic in seeing a drawing of perhaps a long-lost vehicle gradually assume three dimensional

form before your very eyes. Perhaps my best experience of this to date has been in constructing a Festiniog Railway 'curly roofed van'; the recreation of that peculiar and distinctive, but very subtle roof profile in concrete form (not difficult, once you have an accurate working drawing) was quite extraordinarily rewarding. I certainly do not claim that I am producing very finely-crafted models, but that is definitely where I am aiming – and the actual practical process of building such items can be deeply satisfying in its own right. It is also a good diversion when the vagaries of the British weather prevents outside activity; there are people out there who already produce superb bespoke models, the large scale of which simply enhances their beauty as items in their own right.

In this context, reference to the prototype is probably the most advisable route, since the resultant model will be faithful to a completely credible historical item; freelance models may have their uses, but they somehow never quite manage to achieve that same level of credibility, however well they are made. Despite this, some of my models have had adaptations, notably to accommodate some of the operating restrictions that my line imposes. I have, for instance, shortened my L&BR and FR coaches by one compartment in a way that would cause a purist complete horrors – simply to get them round my curves without their either buffer-locking or looking totally silly. One has to be quite careful how this is done – it is best to try to retain the symmetry of the vehicle, and there are some that don't lend themselves, such as the L&B third class observation coaches with their open centre compartment – you can't model half a compartment! I normally produce my full size working drawings on a scanner and printer, and by printing each half of a coach side on a separate sheet, it is possible to 'telescope' the drawing in such a way that you lose the desired amount while retaining as much as possible of the original's character. Another point that could well be problematical for the purist is the issue of livery. I have had few qualms about painting my vehicles in the house livery rather than their original colours; I don't think that it detracts too much form the essential nature of the models, and I was careful to choose a low-key red which was not far removed from a colour that most of my chosen vehicles carried at some point anyway. The slight loss of fidelity is compensated for, in my mind, by the consistency of appearance of

The finished model, photographed in situ, after it had been out of doors for six months. The brightness of the original finish has been toned down nicely by the weather. The real challenge of this building was the roofline, especially as by some accident I managed not to cover all of it in the original photographs. The rear roof section consists of three slopes, the fourth being truncated to accommodate the chimney of the waiting room. Most perplexing until the penny finally dropped. I used real lead flashing in the valleys of the roof; the building sits on slate flag stones cut from an old roof slate - it makes a huge difference to set buildings off on appropriate ground surfaces.

my fleet. The only exception so far has been the curly roofed van, whose original Victorian livery is so splendid that I just had to try to reproduce it. Where I am more careful is in the composition of trains. I don't go as far as maintaining rakes purely from one original railway, but I am careful what I mix with what. While loading gauges and roof lines were far from uniform on many NG prototypes, I believe it is necessary to compose trains that have some semblance of visual harmony, while retaining some consideration of prototype consists. For this reason, I tend not to run FR and L&B stock adjacent to each other in a single train. I am sure there are some who would consider this approach too lax.

THE SOUTHWOLD RAILWAY

But what about garden models of actual prototype lines? As yet, these are very rare beasts indeed, though Stephen Bazire has shown that it can be done, with his model of the Southwold Railway. Although the most accurate parts of his model are indoors, modelled to indoor standards, he has still managed to create a garden railway that incorporates scenes that are recognisably replicas of real places along that line. Perhaps the big impediment is the lack of control that we have over the environment in which we build our models. With an indoor model, one can configure everything from the baseboards up in such a way as to replicate a real location; in a garden, that is nigh on impossible. Perhaps a true-prototype model is just one step too far for that essential imaginative element to permit in the garden setting, particularly given the degree of compression that would be necessary? And then there is the philosophical dilemma of what constitutes 'accurate'? While it ought to be possible to configure the track layout, buildings etc. to a prototype, just what should one do about the planting? Even if one were to attempt to position plants in 'accurate' locations, there is no

guarantee that one could control them sufficiently to retain that prototype appearance. Unfortunately, on this one, Mother Nature just won't play ball!

If there is a solution, I believe it must again lie in the creation of cameos. On even expansive indoor models, the viewer's field of vision tends to focus mostly on small parts of the model at one time. Within this small field, one can then tell a consistent story. Such things are clearly possible out of doors as well, so that even if a model cannot be made to reflect a real railway accurately, if one can identify the key defining locations within that prototype, one should be able to recreate these and produce something that has significant overtones of the original to it – all the more so if they can be configured in the correct sequence along the line. My LBR has not really presented the opportunity to try this out in any sustained way, but the passing station constructed on Phase Three is my nearest attempt, the area around the main building having been inspired by a photograph of the original at Tan-y-bwlch on the Festiniog Railway. Having said this, I hope that some one is going to prove me wrong before very long, by building an accurate reproduction of one of the seminal real NG locations in 16mm live steam; near the top of my list would be Lynton Station (which, given the hillside it was cut into, could be modelled at a very convenient standing height) and Penrhyn Crossing from the FR.

Whatever – but perhaps this is a wish too far – the prototype still remains the essential benchmark if one is intending to produce real narrow gauge atmosphere. One sees lines where the fact that the railway is ostensibly narrow gauge seems to have been forgotten - there are many lines that incorporate features that were rarely if ever found on real narrow gauge lines. Some people use narrow gauge purely for its convenience, in the sense that it requires less room that a standard gauge line, and because ready-made locomotives tend to be cheaper than their standard gauge counterparts; fair enough, but if one is trying to create an authentic narrow gauge ambience, then a degree of reference to the prototype is essential.

Although I am very happy to subscribe to a belief in a 'prototype for everything', there are certain widely committed errors that often help to destroy the narrow gauge character. The most obvious of these is station platforms, and indeed other areas, that look like Clapham Junction at rush hour, in terms of the number of figures and other paraphernalia set out thereon. Personally, I have major reservations about the use of figures on garden railways, but even if one does use them, they should be few and far between, and of course, in positions of rest rather than in frozen action poses. Some items of infrastructure were

Above: Many narrow gauge locomotives are now in far better shape than they ever were during their original working lives. It is important to remember this when trying to reproduce details such as the degree of cleanliness exhibited by *The Earl* in this picture, taken at the 2007 autumn gala of the WLLR. There is still much to observe and learn from a picture like this, though.

Left: Maesffordd shed on Paul Sherwood's railway is strongly inspired by the Corris Railway. Another picture that demonstrates Paul's talent for integrating railway, buildings and greenery into a pleasing and convincing whole, that just drips the atmosphere of those Welsh lines…
Photo: Paul Sherwood

rare on narrow gauge lines, such as footbridges and even full signalling – both were likely to be too expensive for such cash-starved concerns, and light railway status often precluded the need for the latter. Then we come to ornate cast iron lamp standards and signs – again too expensive and consequently rarely found in most narrow gauge settings, but almost a *sine qua non* for garden lines! A happy by-product of my approach is the excuse (as if one were needed) to spend hours sifting through my growing library of books on the prototype – I confess that I am not a lifelong narrow gauge devotee, and my interest has come from my modelling activities, so perhaps I have some catching-up to do, but to my mind, there is not substitute for immersing oneself in the affairs of the real thing to assist with developing 'an eye' for proper narrow gauge practice.

IN THE AGE OF MANUAL-ONLY LOCOMOTIVES, there was a limit to what was possible in terms of a track to run them on. Such locomotives require frequent on-the-spot intervention to prevent them from either stalling or running away. While it is possible with modern manual loco's to 'trim' them and then leave them to trundle around a loop more or less unattended, personally I think I would find this rather dull. I can appreciate the pleasures of simply sitting back and watch the train trundle by, but then we come back to the difference between representational modelling and 'playing trains'. If running the railway comes a poor second to constructing the models, then a simple running circuit may be all that is required in order quietly to appreciate one's handiwork, and I would be lying if I were not to confess that there are times when I wish for something a little more relaxing than the fairly intensive work of running an end-to-end line. But in the general run of things, I tend to seek more

involvement with the running of my models than 'circuits and bumps', something more akin to the experience of a real driver.

The advent of radio control and such innovations as boiler fill systems has, however, transformed what is possible, and with it the scope for the kind of lines we build.

SIZE OF PLOT

With the ever-increasing price of land and the demands for more intensive use thereof, the size of the typical garden gets ever smaller. Modern high-density developments have little more space than did a Victorian back yard, which can present huge obstacles for the would-be garden modeller, especially one who aspires to realism. There are some enormous and highly impressive garden railways, and like most, I instinctively feel that more is better, with attendant dreams of acres of the garden that I will own 'one day' being filled with trains. Certainly, if your interest is in Gauge 1, then you will probably need a large space, since the kind of radii it requires are just not going to fit onto a handkerchief-sized plot. I suppose you could build a 'plank' type shunting layout in less.

The only point at which such issue can be fully resolved is at the point of purchase of the property – and there are, of course, many more complicating factors that will probably take

By contrast, The terrain on this section of Tarren Hendre was gently manipulated by the addition of spoil from the various water features. This has permitted convincingly undulating surroundings as a background for this 'Lady Anne' locomotive belonging to Gavin Robertshaw. The principle of using the maximum possible extent for landscape, and 'thinking big' is surely applicable to smaller sites.

Left: The raw material. This suburban garden dates from the 1930s and consequently is perhaps somewhat larger than those typical of many more recent houses, but in most other ways it is typical of the kind of space in which the majority of people build garden railways. The shape is regular and the topography uniformly flat. In a mature garden like this, I think it is a good idea to try to retain as much of the existing planting as possible, and shape the line around it. The *sumac* and *berberis* plants could be reasonably sympathetic to the railway, and there is definite scope for a peninsula border with track on it incorporating the area where the trellis and birdbath are – the low wall of natural stone also has to be a scenic asset.

Centre: Andrew Coward's garden in South East London is not vastly different in size from the one above, but Andrew has been able to use almost the entirety of the space. In what is a fairly urban setting, he has still created an outlook that should be pleasing to lay-people as well as hardened enthusiasts.

Lower: Laurie Wright faced a major obstacle in his garden in Aberystwyth – namely the fact that it slopes away from the house on a gradient of about 1 in 4. After much planning, he arrived at this circuitous arrangement whereby his end-to-end line drops by over three feet in its length, from the top station, seen on the right hand side of this picture, to the lower station, out of sight top left, which is a very imaginative use of space.

site has more to recommend it than at first meets the eye. Two other considerations may actually be just as important:

1. Length of plot. Railways are inherently linear things, so a small plot that is narrow but long may have more potential than a wider, squarer one. This is indeed my own experience, where the plot I have used has a total length of about 70ft in an 'L' configuration, but a width of never more than 8ft, and mostly nearer five or six. While this is perhaps a little too narrow for ease of construction, it does not present significant difficulties when it comes to running the trains; indeed it saves a lot of unnecessary movement. It is by no means impossible to have several people running trains at once – although it does become a little cosy – and we have had to incorporate passing places for people as well as trains! What is slightly more regrettable is the lack of places for people just to sit and watch the trains. Peter Harling has achieved a similar feat in an even smaller space: his Pimlico Tramway exists in what is effectively a back yard, in a space no more than about twenty feet by nine, and yet it is a superbly atmospheric little line, even if he has decided to use the smaller end of the spectrum in terms of motive power and rolling stock.

2. Dedicated use. If it is possible to allocate a small space specifically for railway use, one may end up with a better compromise than a larger line that is heavily compromised by other factors. Again, this is my experience, and it means that the railway has had almost total precedence in the design of the space. Even in a large garden, this might be a better option than a line that winds across the whole site but which is largely subordinate to it. Quite often, the railway may be able to make use of spaces that are not suitable for anything else.

TOPOGRAPHY

Manual locomotives don't like gradients: they tend to make the readjustment of the controls even more necessary. Of course, real railways don't like gradients either, for the similar reason

precedence when it comes to such decisions. So most of us have to live with what we can get.

Yet a little more thought or experience will reveal that an expansive system may not necessarily be the best; for a start, were one to be able to model a line to scale length, one would have to do an inordinate amount of walking (and perhaps climbing) just to run the trains. What is more, current locomotive technology does not normally facilitate a run of more than about 40 minutes without the need to refuel. (Coal-fired locomotives, of course, escape this limitation). Then there is the huge amount of maintenance that would be required – many times more than a real line would need due to our small railways having to deal with full-sized hazards. So perhaps the relatively small

Careful planning can pay off in the long run. Andrew Crookell's first railway was largely configured for operational requirements, but on his new line, he is planning both that and scenic requirements simultaneously. His painstaking draftsmanship is allowing him to determine key landscape features such as raised planting beds at a stage when they can be integrated into the overall design. Photo: Andrew Crookell

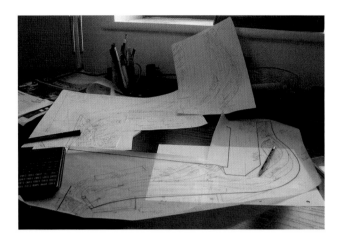

that they led to inefficient and uneconomical use of the power source. Railways in general were built to be as level as the terrain would permit – but it is the latter part of that phrase that is the critical one. Narrow gauge railways were normally built because the terrain through which the proposed route passed was too extreme for a standard gauge line to be economically built. Consequently, most narrow gauge railways exploit the goat-like properties of their engines to climb into places where standard gauge ones simply could not go. The resultant gradients were sometimes spectacular, such as the mile after mile of constant 1 in 50 on the way up to Lynton, or in more exotic climes, the extreme feats of the Darjeeling Himalaya or Guyaquil & Quito Railways. A similar thing could be said about the use of curvature on such lines.

So long as we are prepared to use radio control, this characteristic of the narrow gauge can be used to bring greater interest to even small lines. For example, Roundhouse locomotives will happily climb a 1 in 36 gradient (equal to one inch per yard) and mine are made to go even steeper without undue effect on their performance. In fact, in some ways the locomotives work better under load, and the sight and sound is certainly very pleasing. Coming down again is somewhat trickier, with a train weighing a number of kilograms pushing you onward, and knowing the line as per the real thing, is essential. The weather conditions can also make a difference here, with the challenge of wet rails adding to the interest. Different locomotives may be found to have different load capabilities under such conditions, but what could be more realistic than that? A number of my acquaintances have speculated on the possibility of adding radio controlled braking to vehicles, either the locomotives (which might be tricky given how much other equipment they already cram in) or possibly to brake coaches and vans; at least one modeller has actually built a working wind-on brake in this way. Were this to be under the control of a second person, you effectively create the situation where a train has both driver and guard!

As many a novice has found to their cost, the garden that they perceived as flat is in fact anything but, when it comes to putting a level across it in order to lay a line. As for how many hours and how much material has subsequently gone into creating a many a level track on a sloping site, I shudder to think. Was all that effort really necessary or worthwhile? For those who deal with this problem by elevating their line on posts, there is both a considerable amount of work involved and a considerable impact on the appearance of both the garden and the railway. While one must of course acknowledge the concerns of older modellers who may be less prepared to work at ground level, there have to be other solutions to the issue. In certain circumstances, then, gradients can be the friend of the garden modeller, rather than the foe.

DRY STONE EMBANKMENTS

The ongoing debate about the best working height for a railway is, in some ways spurious. As I said earlier, when real railways rose hundreds of feet up mountainsides, the kind of vertical displacement that we are considering is as nothing. An elevated line even at the height of three feet is raised by not more than

the height of a decent 16mm scale viaduct, or one of the Festiniog Railway's larger dry stone embankments. The amount of vertical variation found *within* a model's parameters normally translates into a matter of not more than about 30 Scale feet. The average modern suburban plot is, of course, unlikely to include any topography at all, which makes the job considerably more difficult – but then presented with such a blank canvas, imposing any character at all is, frankly, going to be a major task. In a small plot, the use of different levels can both add interest to the railway, and sometimes a greater length of run.

Most garden railway planning starts with a decision over where the railway is to run, and then a decision is made of how to form the railway to achieve this. In gardens that do present some height variation, perhaps a better, if slightly idealistic approach would be to decide on the key locations on the line, such as the major stations, and then allow the terrain to dictate the route of the line in the intervening distance – just like the real thing. In this way, earthworks and civil engineering structures would be used as appropriate for the ground being covered, rather than being artificial features introduced just for the sake of it. This may sound extreme, and in gardens which have other uses, there may be areas that are out of the question in terms of railway incursion; it might mean that one loses out on some of the desired features, but this is in fact totally consistent: the routes of real railways were also restricted by factors such as land ownership, and there is nothing to stop you gently manipulating that terrain somewhat to introduce the need for a certain feature. Neither is this an approach suited only to large spaces; my LBR is about as restricted as you can get in terms of ground area, but in fact this simply led to the use of features such as gradients and bridges where on a wider site the line might have simply meandered. The point, however, is the same – my gradients and bridges exist to deal with specific topographic problems imposed by the site, and I have resisted the temptation to introduce unnecessary ones, however much I might want to have a tunnel!

It is important also to consider the scale size of the terrain we are using when it comes to linear planning. Remember that one foot of length represents only twenty or so feet in the real world. How many hillsides with cuttings in them have you seen that are only forty feet long? It may appear that I am forgetting the size constraints of the average garden here, but what I am really arguing for is 'doing less but better'. A cutting or embankment really needs to be a minimum of ten to twenty feet long in order to create any real representation of such, and probably a foot or more in depth to be of a scale that would have justified its creation. Most lesser variations would probably have been surveyed out. I would argue that physical features created simply for their own sake are in danger of looking ridiculous simply because it is unlikely that they can or will be

Left: One can begin to see the way in which the raised height of Andrew Crookell's new line will be used to advantage. There are already some early plants starting to establish themselves in front of the stone built wall, and these will eventually be joined at ground level by buildings and pathways masquerading as roads. The need for a walk-through has been exploited to produce a tall skew bridge in the left-background, utilising Keith Bucklitch's superb 'cast-iron' steel components.

Lower: Civil engineering needs to be done on a scale that avoids the 'tunnel through a mole-hill' syndrome. This cutting on Tarren Hendre was needed to permit the line to drop down through the natural topography of the site – nothing contrived here.

made big enough not to do so. The decision to 'go with the flow' when it comes to topography, and a little will-power in doing without unnecessary features is more likely to yield a realistic result.

SENSE OF ANIMATION

A similar issue relates to the use of water on a model. It is a most attractive feature, providing movement when there is otherwise none, but again it needs to be done with some sense of scale: for example, a harbour will require a considerable expanse of water if it is to look like anything more than a puddle; even a pool will need to be larger than a bucket, and how many railways would then have built a bridge across it? We are here handicapped by the fact that we don't have a convenient baseboard edge off which to 'lose' the rest of the water, but I see little point in pretending we do; better to deploy water in a way that fits the space we have available. A mill pond might be appropriate, perhaps with the railway skirting it; a canal might be possible (though bear in mind that canal basins are large affairs), or perhaps most attractive of all, a running stream, as has been done well by Steve Delarre on his Moreton Pit Light Railway. The sunlight catching running water provides a delightful sense of animation, and what could be more appropriate for the hill-country that many narrow gauge lines inhabited? Failing all else, build an open-topped water tower and fill that! I think that it is far better *not* to do something and find an alternative, than to do it unconvincingly.

We also need to remember the relationship between terrain and our track when laying out a line. True, many narrow gauge lines twisted and turned round outcrops and valleys, but the curvature was still generous in comparison with what we often set

out on our models. Sinuous curves can be very appealing in terms of the movement of a train around them, but roller-coaster-like bends do not achieve nearly the same effect! I almost came a cropper even on my last phase of the LBR by putting in some 'unnecessary' curves in order to create the twisting effect. It just did not look right, so I realigned the track with only a couple of curves, and lo and behold, it looked a lot better. There must be few lines where the 'straight' between two curves was little longer than one coach, and the train looked most peculiar moving along this stretch, not at all the effect that I had envisaged. While curves may be more immediately appealing, straights have their own qualities, for example when seen head-on with a train gradually getting bigger and bigger as it approaches, its waggling gait accentuated by the foreshortening. A straight some twenty or thirty feet long, is by no means over-scale, and in visual terms can in fact serve to accentuate the curves at either end of it.

RAILWAY CIVIL ENGINEERING

What I am arguing for here is not an idealistic situation where we can only produce a realistic effect if we have several acres of undulating ground to play with, but simply that we should 'go with the flow' more in exploiting what we do have; that we should take a holistic view of the topography of what is usually a very small piece of scale terrain at our disposal, and resist the temptation to create tiny hummocks for our tunnels and cuttings to pass through, or puddles to call lakes. You can only shrink reality by so much before it starts to look ridiculous. Natural ground variations will often provide all we need, and if a little manipulation is necessary, then we should do it with regard to the overall scale of the garden and the model that is to go within it. A few lucky people have built their garden railways in locations where they overlook superb distant views, which provide most of the wider setting in the most realistic way of all; the rest of us can always dream! In this way, I believe that it is possible to build a usable railway in such a way that it is a superb asset to its garden rather than the opposite, and one that reflects true railway civil engineering practice in its construction. By doing so, we will make an automatic gain in realism.

There remains in this section, the final thorny question of convenient operating height. I certainly found out rapidly why some people are strong advocates of raised lines! Although I am only in my forties, the constant bending or kneeling down to a ground-level line can be hard work, especially with operations to perform quite regularly on reaching the end of the line. And

it is indubitably true that one can appreciate one's models from a more realistic and satisfying perspective if you are not constantly hovering in a helicopter above them! However, against that, I am in little doubt that a truly realistic garden railway can only exist at ground level. Anything else will be varying degrees of 'baseboard' built to accommodate a model – in the process the line will be divorced from its true natural setting, landscaping it will become more 'forced', and you may well lose the interest of responding to the true terrain of your plot.

I must concede that if all those who have gone before me have failed to solve this issue; then I am unlikely to do so quickly either. In the end, each of us needs to make a decision that is appropriate to our own personal needs, but I still wonder whether we have as a hobby fully explored the full range of solutions. There has been at least one garden railway built on indoor-style baseboards – but one would never have known to look at it, as the entire surface had been planted using pots recessed into the surface, and from close-up this was very effective. I have not seen sufficient pictures of this railway to be able to judge the more distant effect. More common is to build the line on a raised border, a typical height being perhaps one foot, but sometimes more. The scale of the required earthworks may restrict the area over which such an approach can be used, as you need a surprising amount of infill for even a small area. I think that one simple improvement here is to ensure that the railway does not simply run round the perimeter block work of such a border. There is surely more scope for realism in making the line recede into the depths, and at very least, the positioning of some 'ground' on the outer side of the track will embed the line more fully in its setting. Somewhat more demanding, and not often done, would be the masking of the raised section by creating a bank of soil up the side of the block work – perhaps except for places where attention to locomotives would require closer access.

KEEN 'OPERATING' MAN

Andrew Crookell has found a promising resolution of the height issue in the second incarnation of his Dean Valley Light Railway. He is building it on the Lincolnshire Fens – not an area noted for its extensive topographical variation, and certainly a challenging location in which to represent the Welsh uplands! Since constructing his first garden railway, Andrew has, like me, been drawn more and more to the possibilities for authentic modelling, but as a keen 'operating' man, he also needed to maintain good access to his locomotives (one of which is coal-fired) and to track work for shunting.

At his principal station, he decided to retain his raised line approach from his previous model, set up by around two feet on stone-effect blocks, the track bed being gravel boards placed to create a base board. He has, however, incorporated raised borders into the structure so that vegetation can form part of the model, thus integrating the raised section visually into the rest of the garden. Andrew has then gone that crucial stage further by deciding to use the raised section as just part of the topography. Two feet represents just under forty feet at full scale, and given his use of stone-effect edging, this has given the opportunity to create the illusion that the railway has been built on a shelf on a hillside, a situation that existed for example at Corris. Andrew's masterstroke has been to take the scenery down to ground level, even if the track does not. He has placed planted landscape in front of his raised section, and will in

Andrew is also using cardboard mock-ups to arrive at a pleasing and authentic arrangement for the numerous buildings in this quarry setting.

due course add buildings and roads and other features similarly so that the railway effectively runs on a shelf at roof height, in the style of Tanygrisiau on the Ffestiniog Railway.

Andrew had made full use of the gained height to incorporate some impressive bridges, the currently-existing one utilising Keith Bucklitch's steel bridge components to create a skew bridge inspired perhaps by Dolrhedyn Bridge, also at Tanygrisiau. He also intends to bank the landscape up behind the shelf, perhaps as high as several more feet, and this, combined with the use of full scale buildings will in time give the best of both worlds, as well as solving the topographical shortcomings of a flat garden.

STATION AND SLATE QUARRY

Andrew intends that the rest of his new railway will gradually descend on a gradient into a more 'natural' section, with the raised section blending into natural topography. In the fullness of time, he will be able to operate his station and slate quarry at a comfortable height, while also gaining from the less intrusive impact on the garden of the main running line. At the lower end of the line, which will be nearer ground level, it will hopefully be possible to excavate a shallow standing area – the poor drainage of the locality will probably preclude a full-depth operating pit, but a depression of perhaps one foot will nonetheless assist with less strenuous operations.

Another relatively unexplored possibility comes from the previously mentioned issue of the scale vertical dimension. Many narrow gauge lines climbed hillsides along their route, obvious examples being the Talyllyn, Vale of Rheidol and Festiniog Railways. If it were possible to contrive a hillside of this scale, most probably by utilising the topography of a naturally sloping site – the kind of which many garden railway modellers might reject – then building the line on a ledge at a usable height along the slope would solve a multitude of conflicts, and produce a fascinating line that snaked along a ledge in a thoroughly prototypical manner. A model of Abergynolwyn could be built conveniently at chest height!

A final consideration is the possibility of building a servicing pit, with steps descending, which brings critical areas up to a comfortable height. Jeremy Ledger and Andrew Coward have both made effective use of this device, though it clearly involves considerable work, not only with the digging but also to overcome potential drainage problems.

Whatever the specific issues, there is perhaps one key difference when it comes to the two groups caricatured earlier: when planning a garden railway, the engineer will probably start with the railway in mind, and proceed to work out how to adapt the garden to it – while the artist will begin with the garden and seek possibilities for incorporating a railway within its landscape.

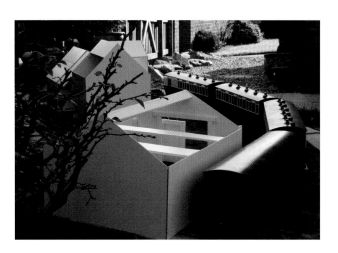

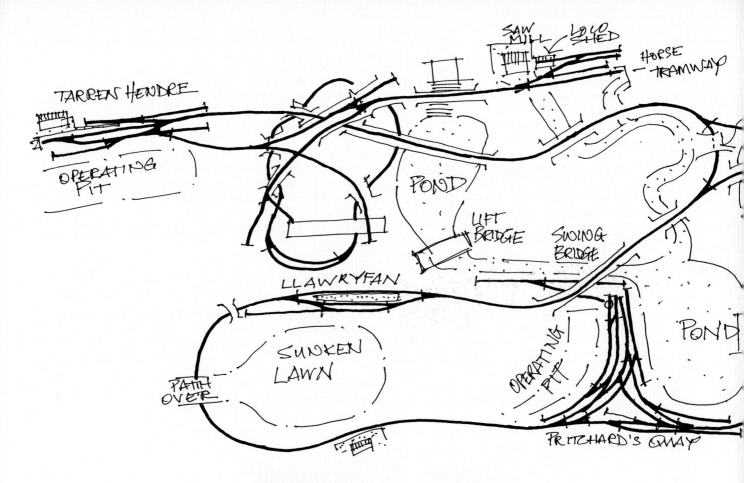

TARREN HENDRE

OPERATING PIT

SAW MILL   LOCO SHED   HORSE TRAMWAY

POND

LIFT BRIDGE   SWING BRIDGE

LLAWRYFAN

SUNKEN LAWN

PATH OVER

OPERATING PIT

POND

PRITCHARD'S QUAY

What & why

By Jeremy Ledger

THE **TARREN HENDRE** came about through a couple of practical considerations combining with a couple of conceptual ones. When I moved from my parents' home into a small cottage with very limited space for an indoor railway, I found I had a fair sized if very derelict garden. At about the same time I was realising that, short of having a substantial barn to build an indoor line in (I was working in 0/16.5 back then), I would never have the space to give me a satisfactory 'journey' for my trains. The Reverend Peter Denny's garden line had captured my imagination many years before and the idea of using the garden itself as scenery for a line of reasonable length was irresistible.

Train journeys to me are 'linear experiences'. They have features and sections with each with its own character, and although I would say this is so of all journeys by train, the shorter self-contained lines such as the Welsh ones bring this out. Take the Talyllyn for instance, from Wharf you start in a cramped site, hemmed in by roads and the Cambrian main line. You pass through the town, hemmed-in by cuttings until you reach Pendre with its sheds and signs of engineering activity. From there the scenery opens out into the vast flat plains with hedges and trees. Then comes the sylvan glade of Rhydyronnen; then Brynglas, which seems so remote and beyond, a different kind of scenery again as the line enters a narrowing valley and gains its shelf on the side of the open hills. This contrasts with the woodland at Dolgoch and the hills close in more and more until the dramatic ravine at Nant Gwernol is reached and then the even more remote tramways to the quarry beyond. No terminus/ fiddle yard layout is ever going to be able to create that sense of transition, so outdoors it had to be. And an end to end line it had to be too, for that sense of having passed from one part of a journey to another is lost entirely if you find yourself passing through the

same bit of woodland and over the same bridge as you did just a minute ago!

Although the Tarren Hendre's route is very short to represent a whole railway (100 yards or so – not much over a scale mile) we decided that we could still get enough of a journey in the length of run to make it work. Some representation of a slate quarry at one end and a harbour/canal basin at the other gives a reason for the traffic on the line to be moving. We also have a sawmill near the quarry; so again, there's a reason for a truck-load of tree trunks to be on the move.

With the acquisition of a piece of isolated wasteland at the bottom of the garden has come the opportunity to take the length of the main line to close to two scale miles which, when finished, I think will improve the impression of the making of a journey considerably, and add some new sections with different characters to make up that experience.

Many garden lines feature stock from all over the world with Darjeeling loco's rubbing shoulders with quarry Hunslets and something that ran in Australia. I can see the appeal, I really can, as there are so many attractive lines and different types of stock, but we have restrained our acquisitions to things that either did, or could have, run on a Welsh quarry line. Inventing a history for a freelance railway is a (much maligned!) pastime in its own right but some sense of how a railway got to be where it is and look like it does is useful to inform choices such as appropriate stock and buildings. The prototype of our Pearse 'Leeds No1' for instance, was built for a dam construction project in Yorkshire and was scrapped for want of a purchaser in the 1930s. She could have been acquired by a Welsh quarry railway – perhaps the Welsh Highland even, given her close family similarities to WHR stalwart

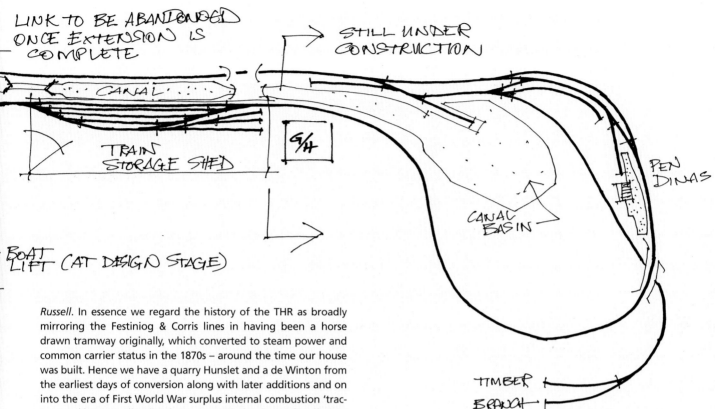

LINK TO BE ABANDONED
ONCE EXTENSION IS
COMPLETE

STILL UNDER
CONSTRUCTION

CANAL

TRAIN
STORAGE SHED

S/H

PEN
DINAS

CANAL
BASIN

BOAT
LIFT (AT DESIGN STAGE)

TIMBER
BRANCH

Russell. In essence we regard the history of the THR as broadly mirroring the Festiniog & Corris lines in having been a horse drawn tramway originally, which converted to steam power and common carrier status in the 1870s – around the time our house was built. Hence we have a quarry Hunslet and a de Winton from the earliest days of conversion along with later additions and on into the era of First World War surplus internal combustion 'tractors' and later, smaller diesels to cope with the dregs of traffic late in the railway's operations. We also have a few 'standard designs' of wagon (most notably over thirty Festiniog 2Ton slate wagons) which would have served the line throughout its steam operated days as well as an eclectic bunch of one-offs which might have been taken over from the quarries the line serves. For coaching stock, much of it could have been acquired second hand from lines dispensing with their passenger services such as the Corris & Glyn Valley or, in earlier and more solvent times, by adding an extra carriage to an existing order from a manufacturer building vehicles for the Festiniog perhaps. It may be thin as a justification but perhaps better than none at all!

The usual period for the line we reckon is 1947. The Victorian infrastructure is largely still there but getting rather tired. It is usually operated by 'one engine in steam', which runs a limited service of mixed trains and doubtless tries the patience of its few passengers by shunting at the intermediate stations and sidings. At other times though, we vary the period such that only stock from a certain date and earlier is available which can add to the challenge, or we can run more intensively if a few people are available to work the traffic.

As yet we have no signals, which is a pity. Again with our 'imagined history' in mind we should have at least some basic signalling to protect the likes of the swing bridge over the canal, the absence of which would be of great concern to the Board of Trade. We have in mind perhaps some archaic looking disc signals, which would fit with the surviving mid-Victorian equipment idea and not look too modern and standardised.

And so to the quest for realism… Realism seems to mean many things to different people and to me it is more of a package than a single definable object. For the Tarren Hendre we are trying to produce a line, albeit freelance, that is built and worked to the rules that would have governed a real line if its type. It needs to have a reason for its trains to run and its trains need to look like real trains that worked that kind of traffic. As far as possible it needs to look right – eventually to the extent that a photograph of it taken almost anywhere at an angle that excludes obviously out of scale features, like a fence or a goldfish, would require at least a second glance to confirm that it is a model not a full sized railway. In 'look-

ing right' there has to be a consistency in the type of stock, the level of detail and the overall finish. The same is true of the scenery and its detailing. There seems no point in having a highly sophisticated and detailed locomotive hauling improbable plain boxes on 'steamroller' wheels or indeed a whole train of immaculately detailed stock running through a blank, bland 'field' of out of scale grass.

Ultimately, it needs to *feel* right as an entity too. Real railways develop a character of their own beyond the sum of their parts; mechanical, human, topographical and historical. Even modern day preserved lines still have their own flavour but that seems as nothing to what is exuded by photographs of them doing their original jobs of work. Hopefully the THR can invoke at least a hint of the character of the working slate lines when they were almost as commonplace and workaday as a Ford Escort or a forklift truck is today. We are a long way from fulfilling that mission, not least in the absence of nearly all the buildings, fencing and other fine details that will be needed to get the appearance convincing but in terms of the all important feel of it, by our own measure at least, we do seem to be getting there.

The construction of the Tarren Hendre began in 1990 and the planning for it a year or two before that. Only relatively recently have we discovered there *was* a horse drawn tramway which served slate quarries on and near the real Tarren Hendre mountain and which ran down to a quay on the Dovey river near the village of Pennal. As yet we know very little about this curious discovery but we shall enjoy finding out a bit more.

The genesis of a garden railway. Jeremy Ledger's Tarren Hendre Railway is probably the best example I have yet found of a narrow gauge garden railway modelled 'in the round'. While the sheer scale of its vision is the first thing that strikes you, Jeremy refuses to compromise his standards, and he has gone a long way to demonstrate that finely modelled detail is perfectly viable in the open air. What better way that to let the creator tell the story himself?

This railway (which you may have seen before) is actually built in a very small, enclosed garden. It is designed as a continuous run for someone who likes to watch the trains go by, rather than short, point-to-point operation. The buildings (and indeed the figures) have a 'cartoon' style that is not to my taste, but the trees, carefully pruned to shape over many years, provide a fairly convincing horticultural infrastructure that, combined with tunnel and cutting, breaks up the comparatively simply layout to the point where a train's progress is indicated by the steam exhaust rising through the trees. Photo: Tag Gorton

RECREATIONAL ACTIVITIES DON'T EXIST IN A VACUUM; in many ways they are as much a reflection of the times as any other aspect of everyday life. Recent trends have had their effect; people have more disposable cash to spend on their hobbies, but less practical experience with which to construct them. More significantly, hobbies are constrained by the space required to pursue them, particularly space-hungry ones such as model railways. In this respect, both indoor and garden modellers are facing a growing shortage of domestic space, and it is becoming harder and harder to find that spare corner (let alone more) in which to follow one's hobby. In the case of garden railways, however, there are additional issues to consider, such as the growing tendency to regard the garden as an outdoor room, in which case its style and appearance may well be unsympathetic to a naturalistically styled garden railway. Moreover, unlike indoor models, garden railways can be physically demanding in their construction, maintenance, and operation, and this needs to be considered while planning. Then there are the limitations of the motive power we use; while locomotive technology is improving all the time, unless you use electric power outdoors, we still do not have anything quite as controllable as our indoor counterparts. Coupled with topographical and domestic considerations, it is clear that the planning and operation of a garden railway need to be considered simultaneously.

While indoor modellers may struggle to find room for a layout (and indeed this was a major factor in my move outdoors),

fewer and fewer people now own a garden, and those who do tend to have less space outdoors than was once the case. Given the large size of our models, we may ironically be no better off in this respect than those who work indoors.

CASH-RICH TIME-POOR

This problem is something of a 'time bomb' which could present some problems for the future of the hobby, because its demographic still tends to be relatively old; what is more, the value of the larger houses that they sometimes inhabit is climbing further and further out of the reach of the younger generation who may have the energy and disposable income otherwise to develop the hobby. Until recently, the outlay required for the necessary equipment and the skills base required has tended to mean that this was a hobby for later in one's life, when the

Right: Not all gardens consist of a rectangle of lawn bounded by fences and flower borders. This is the Scottish National Trust garden at Balmacarra near Kyle of Lochalsh. The point of including this shot is simply to suggest that there are more ways of planting a garden than convention suggests. An area of woodland like this would take many years to mature – but then there are gardens to be found that have indeed been around for forty or fifty years, and which incorporate smaller areas of such environments. A slope like this is just crying out for a line to be cut on a ledge, Talyllyn style, into it.

Centre: Now, while we're dreaming, here's about as unpromising a site as one could imagine. This belongs to the home of some friends in northern Tuscany. I spent an idle day one summer plotting how I could use these terraces to build a quite sizeable railway, and came up with a plan that utilised ledges and spirals to climb from one level to another. The plot is about 120ft from end to end, and some of those terraces rise eight or nine feet from one level to the next, but some are low enough to allow a railway to climb. The main downside was the amount of climbing one would need to do while running the line – no joke in the Italian sun. In fact, this site offered great promise for creating a line that was at the same time both at ground level and a convenient operating height.

Lower: With a backdrop like that, I somehow feel that a Welsh line is not going to work – but what better place to exploit the potential of the Roundhouse Darjeeling Himalaya B Class? Even the climate would be about right; I am not aware that the Italians are seriously into their garden railways, though, so one could expect some strange looks...

financial stresses of raising a family had largely passed, and one had perhaps had the opportunity to trade up in the housing market. This is changing – the general increase in disposable income has meant that people can afford to spend more on their leisure time (or what is left of it) earlier in life, and this has been both reflected in and assisted by the greater availability of commercial products which, while not exactly cheap, are perhaps relatively more affordable than used to be the case.

What is more, the garden railway bug is not predictable in terms of at the age at which it strikes, so those of us still relatively young face the dilemma of how to deal with this while still being comparatively short of resources, especially space. In other words, not only have we become a 'cash-rich time-poor' society, but we are increasingly becoming space-poor as well. How an expansive hobby like garden railways will respond to these changing conditions remains to be seen, but it is clear that 'creative' planning is going to be more and more necessary.

So we return to the fact that most of us are limited in the space available in which to indulge our hobby. One thing in our favour is that garden railways are somewhat better at co-existing with other domestic activities than indoor models, in as much as they can happily wind their way round a garden that is otherwise given over to planting, children's play areas or vegetable plots. However, the need to share visual space with those other uses will require careful planning in order to permit a high level of visual realism. In some ways, however, a conventional garden is the worst place to build a garden railway.

It took a little time to dawn on me that despite having a small and difficult plot, in some respects I was very fortunate: the land concerned was so unpromising in a conventional horticultural sense that there was little point in trying to do much with it. When the penny dropped that I could build a railway on it, there was very little domestic opposition, and I have had to compromise very little in what I wanted to do, other than for the physical limitations of the site – the only real issue being the provision of removable bridges to allow the window cleaner to

position his ladder. And given that the land was disused rather than conventionally planted, neither have I had to compete with giant bedding plants and suchlike, the semi-wild plants and rampant ivy proving a much more sympathetic background for the woodland upper end of my line. From this, we might start be considering what we mean by a garden. The traditional British garden is usually a rectilinear shape, and often consists of an expanse of lawn surrounded by borders of either bedding plants or shrubs. It is normally flat, and may feature some kind of hard-surfaced sitting area at one end. The scope for turning this

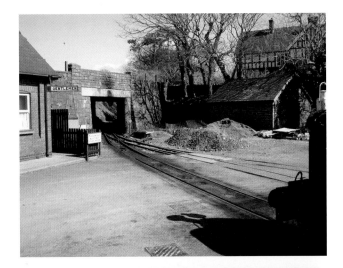

Left: The classic shot of Tywyn Wharf station on the Talyllyn Railway could almost be modelled to full size even in the garden scales, but even if that were not possible, its general configuration, with the helpfully positioned overbridge, could lend inspiration to a small, station based minimum space railway.

Lower: Paul Sherwood owns a moderately sized garden in Norfolk. This shows how well a railway can be integrated into the garden without the need for grotesque structures, and without compromising other uses. This view includes perhaps two thirds of the width and two thirds of the length of Paul's garden, and reflects how creative thinking can arrive at something engaging in even a modest space. Paul has employed a dog-bone type track plan, but curved into a crescent-shaped plot on two sides of his garden.

bring greater interest and a sense of space into small plots. Bedding plants seem to have fallen out of fashion in favour of sculpturally shaped shrubs. While in some ways quite formal, this kind of garden can produce a more naturalistic environment than the traditional bedding plants-and-lawn formula. Of course, this kind of garden is not new – landscape gardening has a long pedigree in its own right, but the looser, semi-wild garden arguably presents the would-be garden railway modeller with many more possibilities; personally, I find the opportunities presented by rock gardens and dry gardens particularly enticing, even if Wales might not be the best prototype for the latter!

In another life, perhaps the ideal place for an outdoor model would be a patch of real countryside, where topography, drainage, geology and vegetation all conspired to provide the most 'real' planning challenge of all; cuttings would need to be cut from real rock and water courses properly bridged; dreaming again, perhaps, but perhaps the inspiration thus provided can be useful on a more sensible level. There are, however, a few places where this has come close to being realised, such as the Llechfan Garden Railway adjacent to Tywyn Wharf Station on the Talyllyn Railway, one example of where a plot of unused land has been given over almost uncontested to a delightful garden railway.

For the rest of us, is it possible to turn the more normal domestic constraints to our advantage? To begin with, the condition of the garden we have at our disposal will be a significant factor. Often, we are not starting from scratch, and will need to work with what already exists; nonetheless, garden redesigns are far from impossible, and a move of house will present further possibilities. Integrating the construction of a railway with a more general garden makeover is quite common – I suspect that long ago, it was discovered that this is an ideal way of calming the waters when such a scheme is mooted!

into a realistic garden railway appears limited, and one is more likely to end up with something that looks like an ornamental railway, like it or not.

A WOODLAND GARDEN

Of course, suburban plots are not the only kind of garden, and where scope and finances permit, this could perhaps be considered at the house-purchase stage. Many older houses possess mature shrub gardens – again sometimes semi-wild, which offer much more promise – and of course we should not completely forget that 'garden' encompasses more than just domestic plots. Were one to be able to obtain a plot with, for example, a woodland garden, the possibilities expand further. The accompanying picture of the woodland garden at Balmacarra near Kyle of Lochalsh might be just a little beyond the scope of many of us, but it didn't stop me having a whale of a time planning trajectories for Festiniog-type forest railway sections as we walked around it! More pragmatically, such an experience does illustrate that certain factors, such as type of vegetation and more especially varied topography (which can be found in smaller sites too) are perhaps more critical than actual size of plot.

However, in recent years, there has been a considerable revolution in garden design; again this has been prompted by the shortage of space and time that many amateur gardeners are experiencing. One of the first casualties was the lawn; it was often replaced with a 'deck' or gravel area, and the shape was loosened up by the introduction of curves, and the insertion of island and peninsula borders, the main purpose of which was to

LIGHT AND SHADE

Even within a modest garden, the dictates of topography can often be a benefit rather than a problem, and with imagination, the general situation of the garden can be made to work for rather than against us. In areas of mature planting, the surroundings may help in the creation of a generally verdant environment in which to run our trains, and in some circumstances, they can even be used as full-size background features. Overgrowing trees may present problems with leaf-drop in the autumn, but they can also provide attractive dappled light to enhance the atmosphere of our models. Damp areas will assist in the growth of 'scale' vegetation such as moss, while light and shade more generally provided by the aspect of the site will create their own atmosphere. Ironically, when I built the third stage of the Lower Bryandale Railway, I welcomed the opportunity to work in a sunlit

This quarry and mill scene on Tarren Hendre could also form the basis for a self-contained minimum space layout, though it might be desirable to add a run-round loop. Some form of run-off for the trains would be needed on the right, whether in the form of storage sidings or a return loop. Given its integration into the surroundings, the height of this section, perhaps four feet, is barely noticeable as you only ever see it from close up (there is a fence close in behind the camera at this point).

area as opposed to the almost permanent shade of the earlier part, but the constant exposure to the sun has actually made it harder to capture the damp atmosphere of North Wales!

Another consideration is the degree of permanence which we expect the railway to have; large earthworks are hard work to construct, and are perhaps best left for times when we expect our model will have a long life-span. In my case, the land used for the railway did not even belong to me, and I therefore initially felt it important to make minimal interventions – just as would many a prototype line, in fact. I evolved a method of track laying that was largely self-supporting, so that block work would not be necessary. A less permanent approach like this will, however, dictate to some extent where it will be possible to lay the track, as there are (probably) limits to the scale of earthworks that can be built up in this way. There are, of course, other more permanent methods of track laying available.

The other issue that needs serious consideration on the planning front is the method of operation of the locomotives. Live steam locomotives in particular, place certain requirements on the driver, and it is no use having even the most superbly realistic railway if it is inconvenient to run. It is necessary to be able to reach the track to rescue trains that run out of steam, to adjust the burner setting and so on. Manual locomotives require even greater access in order to keep them behaving well; then there are the limits to operation imposed by the gas capacity of

the locomotives, although boiler refill valves have reduced the need to shut down a locomotive completely at the end of fill.

ONE-ENGINE-IN-STEAM

When it comes to operating the locomotives, it seems that there is still a general temptation to go for extended running rather than shunting and the other operations that one would see on a real line. This is partly due to the technical limitations of the locomotives, which seem to perform better on long runs, and whose starting and stopping, even with recent technical developments, can sometimes be a little erratic. It is also down to the fact that most of our lines are really so short that we would otherwise be constantly stopping and starting. So even on my end-to-end line, more often than not I simply set out one or two trains and shuttle back and forth on a one-engine-in-steam principle. I think there are a number of reasons for this: firstly the sheer pleasure of watching the locomotive performing, for there seems to be much more reward in this simple pleasure with large scale models than I have ever found with the indoor equivalent. Secondly, there is the constant knowledge that one will eventually need to stop to refuel and therefore one wishes to get the longest run from each session. Thirdly, ground level lines in particular can be quite tiring to shunt, not least because it is less likely that there will be no centralised control point for points etc. so there may be an amount of walking involved, not to mention the constant bending over or kneeling down. This is made worse if you have a radio receiver to keep picking up and putting down - I suspect that manual locomotives make for much more satisfactory shunting. And lastly, at the times when one has visitors, and more than one train may be running, there is the issue of blocking the line for other people.

All of the foregoing militates in favour of a continuous run, which of course gives an infinitely long journey if required. However, realistic it is not. Other than recreational lines, railways normally run from point to point, and even without the

Half a garden shed adapted to create storage area/fiddle yard. This also disguises the continuous run somewhat. Useful where there is insufficient natural height to create a more natural view block.

Buildings used to conceal entrance to 'off stage' area.

Sympathetic treatment of raised front wall reduces its impact.

Even difficult features can be accommodated, in this case a heating oil tank.

Natural materials soften the lines of a very unforgiving background.

Lowered area adds visual variety and creates a useful planting area.

Landscaping in front of track even on a narrow site integrates the line into its surroundings well.

Pimlico Tramway (no passport required)

Seen in rather unforgiving overview, this kind of setting will always be compromised in terms of wider naturalism, but Peter has instead created the possibility for interesting close-ups, whether photographically or in the flesh while the overall effect achieves a pleasing use of a small space – and a snug corner (Lancashire climate permitting) in which to enjoy the railway.

considerations of authentic running, continuous-run lines to me often seem to lack the sense of purpose that comes from having defined 'destinations' at either end. It is more difficult in such circumstances to identify any given point as a sequential part of a route, since there is no clear start and end point to provide locational reference. And not only does this create ambiguity in the running of one's line, for what it is worth, it also makes it more difficult to define the imaginary geography of the line in one's mind. Part of the attraction of narrow gauge lines is their self-contained nature, so this omission seems stronger than it might on a standard gauge set-up, where one could more easily explain away the lack of ends as being part of seemingly infinitely long main line. The ideal, of course, is to have an end-to-end line long enough to accommodate a run equivalent to the longest time for one wishes to drive continuously, but few of us have that luxury.

MINIMUM SPACE

It is probably true that the smaller the site, the more important a continuous run becomes: if your line is only a few yards long, then you may well need to be able to double up and more on that length, at least if you wish to use live steam locomotives. That said modern handsets are becoming smaller, aerials less of a liability, and locomotives more controllable, so a live steam shunting layout would not be as impractical as might be imagined. Perhaps this is also the ideal scenario for those who are devotees of manual control, since the locomotive would rarely be far from reach. One would lose the opportunity for those long runs, but when the alternative is no railway at all, beggars cannot be choosers! Given the sociability of the garden railway scene, longer runs should always be available at others' lines. If your plot is seriously restricted, a model based on one of the Welsh slate quarry or other industrial system, complete with Quarry Hunslets and working inclines could provide masses of potential in a small area. It should be remembered of course, that pro-

ducing a high-detail model is a very labour-intensive task, and in this sense a small model is a very real advantage, as indoor modellers have known for ages.

An inherent problem of this approach is what to do with the trains when they need to move out of the modelled system. I suppose that a permanent process of shuttling wagons around might be one solution, though it is doubtful that it could maintain interest for very long. A fiddle yard does not offer the same opportunities as when used indoors – for a start it would need to be large, and while trains could enter it well enough, the exhaust would be an all too obvious give-away as to the train's whereabouts. Then there are the potential problems of marshalling a hot live steam locomotive by hand ready for the return run – real shunting would probably be needed, and in this case you might as well have it on show on the layout proper.

Peter Harling has used an interesting solution on his small Pimlico Tramway (built into the back yard of an old house in rural Lancashire). He literally cut a small garden shed in half vertically and fixed it to the wall of the yard. Doors now open the shed wall outwards like a large cupboard, and his raised line now runs through this, with storage tracks at running level, and shelves above. The entrances are disguised as sheds and industrial installations and, while much running is circular, it does much more clearly define the 'ends', and provide a good sense of direction up and down the line. It also serves to keep all the usual running paraphernalia tidy in a confined space.

THE CONTINUOUS RUN

Another alternative would be to model a scene part way along a line, with sidings and other features set within a loop, the back part of which is disguised by planting or screening. Thus trains could be assembled and set off down the line, to reappear at the other end as an arriving train, or continue for as many laps as desired. If this is not possible, the departing main line could be made into a simple return balloon loop that returned

trains to the station. This could be as large or small as space permitted and could perhaps make use of an area where scenic development was not possible – perhaps even the area behind a garden shed – and at its most extreme, it could even be a removable trestle. While both of these solutions are moving back in the direction of a larger line, the continuous-run element does not purport to be an entire system – its main function being simply to return trains to the modelled area proper, and therefore it can be as large or as small as space allows, and it could even be fitted non-scenically into inaccessible spaces.

Indoor modellers have increasingly been turning to the idea of cassette storage systems, where the actual 'off-stage' section of the model is small, with trains running onto removable lengths of track, which are then either turned manually or removed to be stored and replaced with another. Given short trains on a minimum-space layout, it might be possible to adopt a similar approach for large-scale models; locomotives would probably need their own, due to their weight, and the system could well be combined with storage cases for them – effectively, the case could have an opening end, and plug directly into the layout. If this system were deployed in a shed or garage, then the visibility issue disappears, and one could integrate such a system with a stock storage area.

One of the things that does become clear with minimum space modelling, is that raising the line up is not just physically more practical, but it becomes visually less of a problem. Running ground-level trains in a highly restricted ground area is hard work – I can speak from experience! What is more, it becomes impossible for the viewer to move sufficiently far away from the model for anything other than a helicopter view to be obtained. The issue of integrating the model with the surrounding terrain diminishes in importance because there really isn't any. In these circumstances, raising the line probably delivers more benefits that it causes problems. To my eye, the most unconvincing raised lines are those that make out across open space since they appear totally divorced from their surroundings. In a confined space, the re-think is total.

CHASMS FOR BRIDGING

Open space is not an issue, and we will only see the model from close quarters, so what goes on below datum level becomes much less important. What is necessary however, is some kind of visual backstop, so that the model becomes in effect a shelf. In many cases, this can be a building wall, but the usual panel fencing could supply a suitable alternative. The 'shelf' could well be built from block work, and be waist-height or more; perhaps attractive brickwork or better still stonework would be more attractive and sympathetic, as again demonstrated by Peter Harling's railway. In these circumstances, the approach is very much that of the indoor modeller, though it should be remembered that the scale height of such a model would present intriguing scope for dropping the datum almost to ground level, to create chasms for bridging.

It might be thought that such a model would present little scope for operation, but at least one modeller of my acquaintance (who has built large layouts of his own), when presented with an extensive line that we were visiting, opted to spend much time shunting the small quarry cameo instead, and came

away completely satisfied! Iain Rice has written much on the design of visually and operationally satisfying small layouts, and he advocates the inclusion of a 'deliberate snag', such as a kick-back siding into the track plans of such layouts; industrial systems would seem to offer masses of potential for this kind of thing. The point of this is to increase operational challenge, and while this may require more thought given the limitations of live steam, the basic notion is surely worthy of consideration. Were one to be prepared to adopt battery or even track power, then such an approach loses little of its indoor applicability. All of these ideas derive from indoor practice and appear not to have been used much out of doors, but perhaps they represent a point where, despite the good-natured condescension that many large-scale modellers show for 'electric mice', we do have something to learn from indoor experience. I concede that they all lose one big attraction of garden railways, namely the notional modelling of an entire line, but they retain most of the other benefits of outdoor modelling, and as I said before, with property sizes shrinking, can beggars afford to be choosers?

MEDIUM SPACE

For those with somewhat more space at their disposal, the traditional configuration of a garden line becomes more feasible. Yet, if anything, more pitfalls lie in wait given more space, perhaps because it is possible to be rather lazier with one's approach and still 'get away with it'. In the normal suburban garden, convention suggests that one build a line around the perimeter of the lawn; it provides close-on the maximum length of run in a smallish area and also ensures that the railway does not conflict with other uses of the space. It is also potentially the recipe for the dullest railway possible, as it is likely to omit many or all of the aesthetic tricks that we can deploy to add interest. At its most basic, on this configuration a train is likely to follow a route described by a series of more-or-less straight lines punctuated by some improbably tight corners at each extremity of the garden, and it will probably never be lost from sight. In that alone, we have left out two of the key ingredients in adding interest – even if I am exaggerating a bit.

The understandable desire for extended running is likely to produce a design that incorporates a continuous run, but much can be done to break up the uninteresting appearance of such a design. The most obvious of these is to place the railway on

The constraints of shape and size fall upon almost all of us. Tag Gorton's small garden limits what can be done in terms of operation and he has indulged his imagination with perhaps a representation of how he would have liked things to have been rather than how they were.
Photo: Tag Gorton

Simple locomotives running a short train in a very confined space – however this railway has atmosphere in spades. Perhaps railway modelling in the garden is more of an art than anything else…
Photo: Peter Harling

an 'island' within the garden, and view it from the outside. If the garden is big enough, the inside view can still be maintained as well, retaining a central lawn area if that is needed, but this will open up a multitude of different viewing points, and given considered planting, the two tracks need not be viewable simultaneously.

With slightly more space again, it may become possible to zone the garden more completely, and bring the railway down the central dividing lines between the sections. A railway configured in an 'S' or 'Z' formation can make use of this arrangement.

What we are discussing here is not railway design so much as garden design. Anyone with even a slight interest in such matters will be aware of gardens that they have seen that somehow 'work' in aesthetic terms, while others in similar spaces appear much less interesting; this holds whether or not there is a railway involved. What we can harness, however, is the potential of the railway to improve the attractiveness of the garden as a whole rather than the opposite – surely a significant gain should one be facing a sceptical 'Significant Other'.

TRAINS DISAPPEAR

One of the key principles here is the control of vistas. Consider the impact on a fairly ordinary landscape snapshot of framing the view with some foreground trees, or the doorway of a building. Similarly, consider how much more inviting home interiors can look when glimpsed from outside, than if one is actually in the room. The ability to restrict, frame and add depth immediately stimulates the imagination to contextualise the view, and to extrapolate from what the eyes are seeing in a way much less possible if one can already see the whole. On my own line, the shortage of space appeared to restrict my options, but I was able to present passers-by with a depth of field of

over forty feet, and this was enhanced by the 'frame' created by the building side and adjacent hedge into a 'portrait' shaped view that emphasises length over breadth; from their perspective, the line and trains disappear almost as far as one can see; I believe it is no coincidence that one of the most-asked questions is how much further the railway extends round the back of the property – such is the power of the curious imagination.

Given the proximity of my line to the building, I also had to consider the appearance of the line from indoors; one is effectively presented with a series of framed images of the line as one moves from room to room. I found I could even use non scale plants, carefully positioned to enhance this idea, whilst also screening one part of the railway from another so as to prevent too much of it being visible at one time.

Placing the railway on a carefully planned island border means that the whole of the line is much less easily seen from any one place, so again the imagination will get to work. This is all the easier if the railway can be made to navigate a peninsula, effectively folding back on itself, with the central 'spine' disguised in some way. This has the additional benefit of extending that all-important run, while again having an effect on the wider garden design by restricting the end-to-end view and frequently increasing both the apparent size and visual appeal of the plot. Another side effect is the ability to use a much more natural route for the line, with generous (by model standards) curves and a less obviously contrived trajectory. Paul Sherwood has adopted exactly this approach on his Maesffordd and Nant

Gorris Railway; built into a modestly sized Norfolk garden it feels much larger than it really is, and has an enlarging effect on his garden as a whole.

COHESIVE AND REALISTIC

An implied part is such a plan is the manipulation of the topography of the garden. While the adding of extra height to even a small garden requires a surprising amount of fill, the possibilities of subtly accentuating higher or lower areas can add more vital visual interest, and sometimes the two approaches can be balanced in the same way that real railways balance the spoil from cuttings with the infill needed for embankments. Failing that, have a few tonnes of topsoil delivered! The key to successful use of this technique remains in doing the work at the most expansive scale possible. Due to our low viewpoint, we tend to over-compress topography in our minds: the gradient on even steep hillsides is normally far less severe than we tend to estimate, the lateral extent of landscapes far greater in relation to their height than we think- just look at some aerial photographs to see what I mean, and avoid mole-hill tunnels at all costs! Keeping angles low (except of course where rock pierces the surface) and planning the topography of the line as a whole, rather than as a set of isolated features, will present a more cohesive and realistic effect.

However, having just discussed manipulation of topography, I think it is generally more convincing to 'go with what you have got' – the creation of a completely artificial landscape rarely looks convincing, in addition to being very hard work. This is perhaps a case of 'less being more' – if the terrain is too low to justify a tunnel, then resist the temptation rather than 'manufacture' a reason, other than in extreme close-up, the deception will just not work. Likewise, use bridges and embankments where the terrain dictates not just because you fancy having one! Laurie Wright's Cwmcoediog Railway in Aberystwyth is one of the most convincing applications of this approach that I have ever seen. His garden initially seems about as unpromising as one could find – it is on a 1 in 4 slope. However, Laurie devised an ingenious plan that permitted a line that drops on about 1 in 50, with use of embankments and cuttings much like the real railway, and he has used tunnels and bridges for exactly their intended purposes of piercing terrain that would otherwise be un-crossable. His tunnels are also the means by which his garden path genuinely gains height, and they have a realistic cover of 'land' above them, rather than just a few scale feet.

I would also urge further consideration of end-to-end plans. On even a modest plot, the loss in tail-chasing ability is offset by a much more realistic feel to operations, though I will admit that running end to end is a less relaxing option, because of the more frequent attention required, and the need to run round the train at each end. The Lower Bryandale Railway is of necessity an end-to-end line, and despite my original misgivings, I doubt that I would now ever plan a simple continuous run. In its initial form, the line was just over thirty yards long, and again more by chance than design, the two termini were close though not adjacent to each other. This meant that, while the two stations did not interfere with each other visually, one could despatch a train from one terminus and, while it was travelling move easily,

It always looks more convincing if the railway can be integrated into the real topography of the garden. Now here is a *real* use for a tunnel! Laurie Wright needed to use them to lose height rapidly on his Cwmcoediog Railway, but the garden path still needed to be kept at a useable gradient; result – a functional tunnel with a good cover of land above it.

ready to receive it at the other. The line was basically a 'U' shape on a plot about 6ft wide (when running one section, you had your back turned on the other track immediately behind you) which widened to about 8ft at the end where the return curve was. A 3ft radius curve was about as tight as reliably workable, though I was able to run 18in-long bogie coaches around it without too many practical problems, provided slightly longer than usual coupling chains were used. This length of run was reasonably engaging, though I did leap at the opportunity to extend when it arose.

THE TWO TERMINI

The short run was enhanced, again of necessity, by the steep gradients, which meant that a driver really did have to know the road, otherwise he would either fail to make the climb to the top terminus, or over-shoot the passing station at the half-way point on the way down! The passing loop, with its own siding was essential, as it made two-train operation possible, and the option to shunt the siding served to extend the end-to-end running time when needed.

Rolling stock was usually positioned in various places at the start of a session, so that there was traffic to move around the system as the sequence progressed. On several occasions, four people were kept fully occupied running this small system, even if space was a bit tight! The same configuration has been kept with the expanded system, the main advantage being a run extended by about another 65ft. The tightest curve has been eased, the passing station re-sited and enlarged, but it has retained its siding, while the original was demoted to a halt. The line is now 'L' shaped, though still on a site never more than 8ft wide, and the fact that it curves round the side and end of my home means that the trains now do go fully out of sight, no one location being able to see the whole line in a single view. The

Track bed

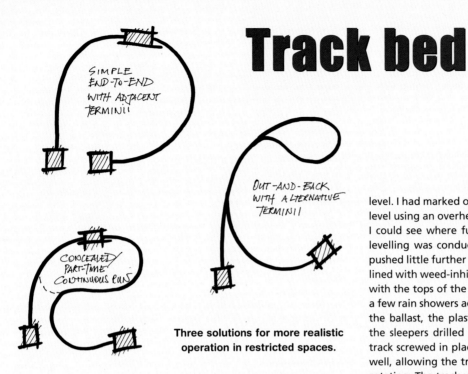

Three solutions for more realistic operation in restricted spaces.

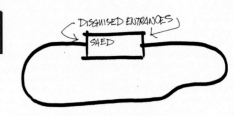

Disguised continuous run
(with apologies to Peter Harling).

LAYING TRACK CAN BE DIFFICULT in a temporary situation. In the early days of the LBR I was not prepared to dig foundations on land I didn't own and so I developed my own method. This involved cutting lengths of 15mm copper water pipe, each about 30cm long, and plugging one end with a wooden dowel, hammered in place and secured and sealed at both ends with epoxy resin adhesive. The track bed was prepared simply by levelling the soil, and where necessary, small embankments were built up with more soil, the sides stabilised by driving in broken pieces of roof slate on edge parallel to the track. The copper 'piles' were then also driven into the ground at approximately 50cm intervals and levelled by using a metre-long spirit

level. I had marked off the maximum permitted gradient on the level using an overhead projector pen prior to starting work, so I could see where further earthworks were necessary. Further levelling was conducted using the spirit level, and piles were pushed little further in where necessary. The track bed was then lined with weed-inhibiting matting, and primary-ballasted level with the tops of the piles, using 'green' alpine grit (which after a few rain showers actually turns out grey). After tamping down the ballast, the plastic-sleepered track was placed in position, the sleepers drilled through into the wooden plugs, and the track screwed in place. The heavy clay of my site held the piles well, allowing the track to be screwed down without the piles rotating. The track was lifted slightly to allow the ballast to be further compacted underneath it, and then a second pour of ballast brought it up to sleeper-top level, brushed into place using an old dustpan brush. This gives a realistic-looking track bed, which actually functions like the real thing, and that has now survived well outside for three years. It does require some maintenance, notably the occasional replenishment of the ballast, especially to avoid slight sagging of the track between piles, which has the effect of producing 'hard spots' in the ride; but generally this technique has served me well. More recently, I have used block or brick track beds simply to increase the noise level of the passing trains, and as my confidence in my neighbours has grown, but the earlier method still works where semi-permanent solutions are required. It should be noted that this technique is probably not suitable for wooden sleepered track, which lacks the strength of a sleeper web to support it.

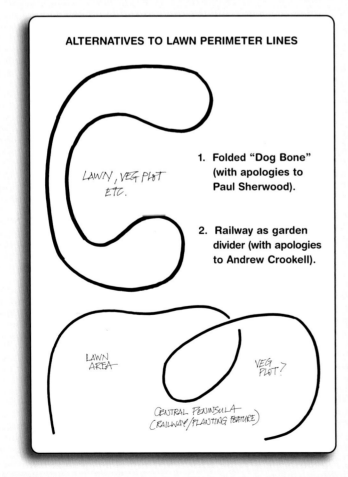

ALTERNATIVES TO LAWN PERIMETER LINES

1. **Folded "Dog Bone" (with apologies to Paul Sherwood).**

2. **Railway as garden divider (with apologies to Andrew Crookell).**

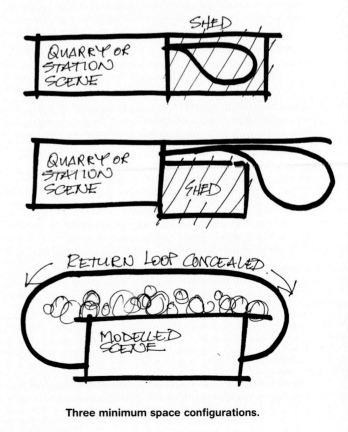

Three minimum space configurations.

The present version of Queen's Forest Road, as seen by a fitter repairing the valve on the water tower. One of the delightful things about a garden railway is the way in which it evolves over time. Some four years after the line was started at this point, I was able to replace the original building with something much finer, and relay the track using only small, alpine grit ballast. The curves into the sidings were also relaid on a better alignment - but keeping the outermost siding, where I had lazily dropped the track down on the bare earth, only for it to be claimed by moss, small stones etc. and end up looking like an abandoned slate siding. This long view of the station also accentuates the tall-tree effect of that privet hedge that first got my mind racing, and this combination of chance and amendment has culminated in what is one of my favourite parts of the line - and all in a space just five feet wide...

completeness of non-communication between the two termini and the mid-way station means that I have had to introduce a train staff system for days when we have more than one train in steam! This 164ft line is mostly plenty adequate in terms of sustained running, especially as the gradients are now even fiercer, and there is more visual diversity in the character of the line. Given the need to run round and perhaps pick up or drop off vehicles at either end, shunt the mid-way siding, and perhaps wait to pass at the mid way point, a round trip can take a surprisingly long time.

However, perhaps the best of both worlds is the line that incorporates a continuous run, with two termini on opposing spurs. In the event of my ever having a garden big enough to present real planning choices, I will probably opt for an adaptation of this. The ideal would be to build an end-to-end line where at some point the route passed close to itself, but on either side of some kind of visual block. This could be topographical, but more likely either a planted border, or a path running between the two sections. In this configuration, two strategically positioned points would lead to spurs that could be connected with a length of temporary track for those times when I wanted a continuous run; the rest of the time it would function as an end to end line. Making the link line permanent but masking its true nature can achieve a different emphasis. In this way, the run between the termini can be extended by multiple laps of the circuit, though personally I have misgivings about seeing the train passing through the same stations multiple times. Depending on space, the relative length of the circuit and the two spurs to termini could be adjusted to taste and if possible, any intermediate stations positioned on the spurs rather than on the loop.

A third alternative would be to have an out and back system in the form of an elongated letter Y, with a return loop at its foot. The multiple passing of stations could be avoided by situating the two termini on the arms of the Y, so that a true end to end run was possible, while if a mid-way station were situated on the return loop itself, all stations would be visited only once, even though the plain track was covered twice, effectively doubling the length of the run without too many visual compromises. Yet another option would be to provide an avoiding line for the intermediate station, but now we are starting to talk about the kind of space required for actually quite a large system.

MAXIMUM SPACE

If you have a really large space available in which to build a railway, the issues change considerably; quite apart from the temptation to look 'up' several sizes to ride-on railways, the main issue becomes how to cope with such a large project, especially if you will be working single-handed. This is not an over-statement – I for one underestimated the amount of labour required for building and maintaining even a small line, and this could become potentially overwhelming when the extent of the railway increases. Despite this, there seems to be embedded in human psychology the temptation to aspire to ever More; but how many dream projects have come to grief because the reality was found to be unmanageable? Even a man of the experience of the late David Jenkinson found that he had bitten off more than he could chew when he started work on his 'Little Long Drag' Settle & Carlisle based 4mm scale railway, and it was never finished.

In the case of garden railways, the temptation is even stronger, because the terrain already exists, and it is all too easy to find new corners of the garden which would make enchanting railway cameos… But here is the rub: even on a large railway, we tend to focus our attention down onto small areas where the action is happening – and just how many of those do you really need? The longer the line becomes, the greater the risk that parts of it will start to function simply as scene joiners, either because the spaces that they occupy are marginal and not suited to full-on scenic treatment, or simply because there isn't the time available to make them anything more. It is perhaps understandable that one might look for a line which is long enough to achieve that sense of purpose which comes when not only are both ends of the line out of sight, but you cannot see much of the rest of the route either. Just like a real railway, this can only really be achieved in a space big enough for the railway really to go from somewhere to somewhere. Then there is the peculiar sense of 'connectedness' that a real railway has – the way in which it creates a linear narrative from what is actually the crossing of an areal expanse of land, the way in which each element in the story is linked seamlessly to those that come before and afterwards – and you need a fairly long stretch of track for that really to come about. A larger plot is also more likely to come with its topographical variation built in – and which presents that fascinating opportunity for the would-be miniature civil engineer.

However, if you took this to its logical conclusion, just how long would the ideal garden-scale line be? To return to my earlier notion of modelling full-size a real railway, perhaps half to one mile long: given that you are not actually riding on the train, how long would you ideally run for before repetition – dare I say boredom – set in? How much of an uninterrupted run is really needed between the places where the action really happens – the sheer pleasure of running the trains notwithstanding? How much walking and climbing do you really want to do in the course of an afternoon's running session? And that is without considering the still quite restrictive technical limitations of most of our models in terms of duration of run. I suppose that long continuous runs may answer some of these questions; especially with the function on more recent control systems to turn off the transmitter and run on 'cruise control', one can

Andrew Coward's Isle of Westland line is what I would consider to be a medium-space line, and is perhaps typical of the older suburban plot. Andrew has luckily been given an almost free run of the entire garden, and his love of planting has resulted in a railway that looks much bigger than it actually is. Notice the use of a very discreet operating pit to allow the station to be run at waist-height without compromising the ground-level line.

leave the train to run itself for long stretches of the line and just watch, but my own instinct in large garden would be to provide an end to end line that captured the correct feel of that configuration without compromising length of run so much.

A More Practical Solution

Trying to offer some figures, the thirty yards of my original LBR was too short; the present fifty is better, given that it is a tricky route to drive. Jeremy Ledger's one hundred and twenty or so yards is better still, giving the feel of really undertaking a journey. Multiplying up the typical distance run around a continuous run before the wish for a change sets in, perhaps three hundred yards would be the maximum one might really wish to run at a single time – but what a task to maintain so much! Perhaps a better solution in a large space would be to give part of it over entirely to the railway – a Railway Garden in the tradition of the formal garden, the kitchen garden, the water garden and so on. In that way, life could continue elsewhere, and the fortunate individual would be left to indulge his dreams, free from the ever-present dangers of meteorite-sized footballs, thirty-foot high leeks and day-glow bedding plants…

Given a run of that length, much consideration would be needed as to its overall trajectory. Two termini three hundred track-metres apart would be highly inconvenient to work with steam unless it was arranged for supplies of water and gas to be permanently available that points along the line, and from a communication point of view; a more practical solution would be where the line described an out and back route, or was folded over on itself, with the ends reasonably close together.

One needs to consider whether it will be possible or practicable to model the whole line in the sense intended in this book. The amount of work would be phenomenal and one would again risk ending up with an enormous model village (in the negative sense). There is also the issue of balancing the railway against the full-sized landscape – which is likely to contain considerably sized plants including real trees. A number of workers have suggested that the way forward is to create a series of cameos on which close attention is focussed, stations being the obvious example, but then to link them with track where little or no attempt is made to create a scale landscape, and the line runs for all intents and purposes through a real-scale garden.

On the other hand, large spaces can obviously provide just what is needed to create some really impressive terrain, with height variations measured in numbers of feet rather than inches, and perhaps large expanses of water. Folding the line over or back on itself would be a practical help here – the area of terrain to be created would be reduced by perhaps 75%. However, it would need to be done subtly, especially if an end to end route were being used; while points where lines cross over themselves on bridges can be appealing in their own right, there have been very few places in the UK at least (other than the Dduallt Spiral) where this happened. Bringing two different points along the route into quite such obvious visual proximity does rather destroy the illusion of trains actually travelling from A to B; if the lines must cross, a tunnel would be more successful at disguising the lower route.

Single Line Occupancy

From an operational point of view, a large railway does present opportunities for more people to be involved simultaneously without falling over each other, and there exists that wonderful possibility of waiting peacefully with one's train at a remote passing station for one eventually to appear out of the distance coming the other way. I am going to say little about the headache of managing single-line occupancy when such distances are involved! But there is also the risk of people becoming isolated from each other, wrapped up in their own little world, at which point one wonders what happened to the sociability of the hobby…

I have no personal experience of building or maintaining a large line, but I have run on a sufficient number to start to encounter the issues – which is not to say I wouldn't leap at the opportunity to build one if it presented itself! It is clear, however, that a different strategy is needed. I will therefore leave it to others with more relevant experience to describe. Most modellers will be more preoccupied with the other end of the scale.

Whatever the size of the model, an important tool is to have a 'story' for one's line. I am not referring to the elaborate mock-histories that some devise for their railways, but at least a loosely defined *raison d'etre* for it. The hackneyed one, of course, is the Welsh slate-carrying line, but there were plenty of other uses of narrow gauge railways, if this does not appeal. Failing all else, one can explain the railway as a tourist line built to open up areas of scenic beauty. But whatever the plan is, it will provide a framework for making decisions in such a way as to provide a general consistency of approach, from the basic plan to localised detailing, from the architecture to the trains that will actually run and their main cargo.

There is something enchanting about the sight of a model steam locomotive moving through one's garden; whether your personal preference is for the mechanical or artistic side of the hobby, the end result rewards careful consideration of the options available. Breaking the rather unimaginative orthodoxy in this aspect can lead to superb results, and while taking part in circular processions at open days has its attractions, the benefits of a more complex and realistic approach to running one's line should not be underestimated. The sight of a train moving realistically through convincingly scaled terrain never ceases to fascinate me; one could almost be sitting on a distant hillside watching the real thing – and that for me is what it is all about.

IF THERE IS ONE THING that 'grabs' me about a good garden railway, it is not the quality of the engineering, or even the live steam traction, but the overall atmosphere that it creates. This is barely even an aspect of railways but more to do with gardening. I am no great horticulturalist, but I have spent some pleasant hours of my life exploring various gardens – enough to know that, on an atmosphere front, there are some that 'have it' and some that don't. I must confess that these days, imagining how a garden railway could be fitted in augments such exploratory pleasures – I have great plans for Kew! I don't think one has to be a hardened railway enthusiast to understand that a garden railway can provide an intriguing focal point for a garden, and I have had numerous gardeners stop to discuss my railway along with all the railway enthusiasts. We come back to the sense of theatre that railways can engender – the intrigue of a small line disappearing into the vegetation, and the movement that the trains can bring to an otherwise often static scene. Considerations like this are very useful in the necessary negotiations with other members of the household when mooting one's first line. Hopefully, from then on, they won't need further convincing…

Achieving atmosphere is where our device of having a story for our railway comes in useful again. Knowing at least the general geographical setting and possibly more, will help us to make decisions regarding what we put into the model with a little more rigour than spur-of-the-moment appeal. Some people 'locate' their models in distant places, myself included, though there is something very appealing in the alternative, which is to situate it within one's actual locality. Doing the latter will mean that the general surroundings and even climate help to create an authentic regional atmosphere. Those fortunate people who live in North Wales don't realise what advantages they have! This is one example of how following the conventional wisdom

led me a little astray; unlike my indoor models, which have always been very firmly geographically rooted, I started without any clear identity in mind for my line. It gradually assumed a Welsh identity, though I feel that this does not come through as strongly as it might despite the later addition of more distinctive regional features.

This is not to say that it is impossible to create a regional atmosphere elsewhere, for there have been a models that do this very successfully; both Paul Sherwood's and Jeremy Ledger's railways, for example, are very convincingly Welsh, though it is perhaps no coincidence that one which simply oozes Welsh atmosphere is Laurie Wright's line – situated in Aberystwyth! In my own case, the physical conditions are not right for a Welsh line, vegetation doesn't grow sufficiently abundantly on my plot and the space simply isn't large enough for a real evocation of the Welsh countryside.

MORE CONVINCING

I have made much of the similarities that exist between aspects of indoor and outdoor model railways, but scenery – or perhaps I should say the landscape – is one of those areas where the differences are greater than the similarities. It is also an area where I think we have progressed least far in terms of sophistication, or in finding out just what is possible.

I think it is clear that realistic landscaping of a garden railway is going to work in a completely different way from its equivalent on an indoor model. It will present many more problems but

A shot included for the pure pleasure of seeing a well-modelled landscape. A train of visiting LBR stock heads coast-wards on Tarren Hendre. Photo: Gavin Robertshaw

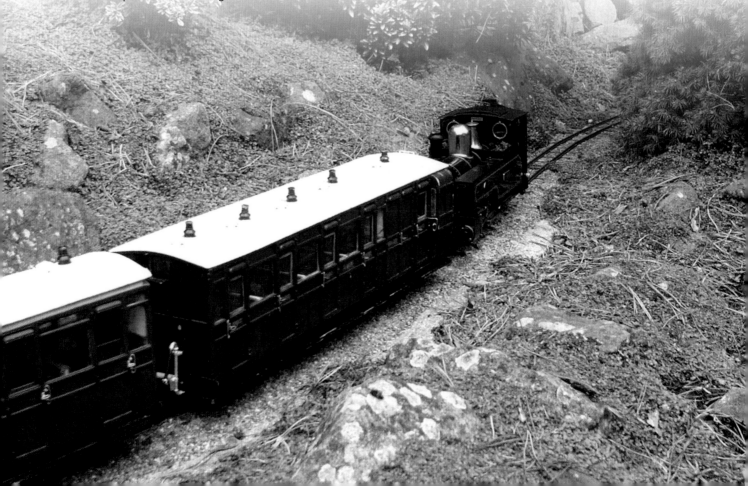

I was pretty pleased with the landscaping on my small *Kenmore* OO finescale indoor layout, built over the winter of 2007-8 when the weather was too bad to go outdoors – but it doesn't even come near the equivalent work on Andrew Coward's railway. This is where garden railways part company with indoor models, and I think it is pretty clear who is the winner. While real planting may technically be out of scale, sensitive treatment and the use of 'drift' planting ensures that the overall effect does not jar. What is more, the landscape is living, and my picture cannot, of course, show the 'trees' moving in the wind…

fact that, by some mysterious part of our empathy with nature, we tend to accept 'growing things' as they are, without particularly attempting or needing to scale them against human objects. Thus it is possible to use full sized plants to create a landscape even though they are grossly out of scale both in terms of their overall size and the size of their individual leaves. I think there are two factors to consider here.

MAJOR SCENIC FEATURE

Firstly, we must return to this issue of field of vision. When we focus on something relatively small, low down and close up, such as a garden railway, we immediately remove from view a lot of the surrounding garden. In this way, the major 'scenic feature' of my original railway was the eight-foot-high privet hedge that runs along the edge of the plot. In 16mm scale, these bushes work out at about 160ft high – rather larger than most British vegetation, even though it should be borne in mind that a fully mature tree could work out at 4-5ft high in 16mm scale. However, in railway terms, the only bit that really mattered was the wizened stems of the bushes, which provide an admirable representation of a line of gnarled old trees, and the lowest couple of feet of vegetation; beyond that, it doesn't really matter how high the plants are as they are out of sight, and given the smallness of my plot, I never get far enough away from them for them really to jar.

Secondly, there is the fractal nature of Nature. This refers to the fact that many natural patterns repeat themselves at various scales of magnification, so that, for instance, a lump of rock is effectively the same thing at any scale, its texture, undulations and colouring being simply those of a pebble or a boulder depending on what scale you want to measure it against. Plants work in a similar way, most obviously through the dendritic pattern of their trunks and branches, which is endlessly repeatable – more or less why Nature chose it in the first place! While some plants scale down more easily than others, we can use small bushes to represent large trees, and likewise spreads of leaves can be used to represent larger versions of the same thing. Rather more inexplicably, even large-leafed plants don't clash irredeemably, as the mind seems to be capable of readjusting the perspective to assume that they are simply nearer to the viewer relative to the model than is actually the case; after a certain point, plants also cease to be a set of individual leaves and just become a general green shape, in which the size of individual parts diminishes in importance. Having said this, it is a generally accepted wisdom that it is better to keep larger leaved plants further away from the railway itself, if only for photographic purposes.

Yet despite this helping hand that Nature lends us, it is far from inevitable that we will get it right. As with many aspects of garden modelling, conventional thinking seems to be focussed on overcoming what we have been bequeathed, rather than working with it.

A major problem here comes from the multi-use nature of most gardens. As I have said elsewhere, in some ways, they typical garden is the worst place in which to build a garden railway. Add to

the potential is there to create a landscape far and away more convincing than any indoor model, if only because it has one key advantage – life. It will be a lot less possible to produce an accurate scale landscape for our trains to run through because we are effectively working with 12in to 1ft materials, and only some of them will be sympathetic to scaling down. However, I think that it is nonetheless possible to produce a convincing landscape for our railways, even if it is not an accurate scale reproduction.

Historically, the model engineering side to our hobby paid no more than lip-service to landscaping of the line; some unfortunates were required by the domestic authorities to plant hedges or build walls to screen the visually intrusive effects of their tracks on stilts. Others simply didn't bother, relying on the fact that their lines ran through areas where things grew to provide the dim background awareness of 'countryside' that was all they needed. In one sense, that approach can lend us one thing – the

Left: One of those 'golden moments' on the real thing: a tranquil moment at Dolgoch as an afternoon train pauses on its way up the valley to Abergynolwyn. Only a garden railway could hope to capture the conditions that are the making of such a moment.

Right: A tranquil moment at Minffordd (LBR) as an afternoon train pauses on its way down the valley to Castle Bryan.

this the multiplicity of priorities that people have for the railways themselves and there is plenty of scope for failure on this front.

To begin with, most gardens are family spaces, where the requirements of children and partners will need to be considered. This may mean that recreational spaces and equipment will intrude into our miniature worlds, as may vegetable plots or conventional flowerbeds. If one's garden consists of traditional areas of bedding plants, it is going to be quite difficult to achieve scenic realism as the steamers chuff their way between serried ranks of begonias and pansies! Yet quite reasonably, this type of planting is a requirement that many people have of their gardens; this is why it might be advisable to try to allocate a separate section of the garden for each use, which is after all a traditional way of zoning garden space. If space were very short, perhaps height separation of the two uses would be possible. Ultimately, the resolution to such dilemmas will be down to the individual's negotiating skills.

ARCHITECTURALLY OR CULTURALLY

Equally, there are some garden railway enthusiasts who build lines primarily for their decorative or 'entertainment' function – as a 'garden feature', and again, the relationship between the railway and the garden will be very different from that of scale realism, with any representation of the railway's surroundings being at most symbolic or even tongue-in-cheek. I am not decrying

these approaches, though I will admit that they do very little for me personally, and given that the compromises they imply will largely be accepted by those who choose such an approach, I feel they are really beyond the scope of this book.

Just to be contrary, I find that highly modelled miniature landscapes are not entirely appealing either. While a model village approach to garden railways can be very charming, it quickly descends into tweeness. While the best model villages, such as that at Bourton-on-the-Water are both impressive and atmospheric, the majority are more of a symbolic representation of reality than anything very realistic in themselves. To be fair, they often don't set out to be anything else – a cross between entertainment and a collection of architecturally or culturally significant buildings – but the purpose is usually to display the building rather than create a realistic ensemble. A number of modellers have experimented with the possibilities of pruning suitable species to look like miniature trees; sometimes it works well, but it probably takes a lot of practice to end up with something that looks naturalistic and not simply a form of miniature topiary – and it is also a very high maintenance approach.

My personal quest is to arrive at something between the two: a scene that makes reference to the models that run through it without becoming a fully-fledged miniature. I envisage a planning process that is able to consider both the 12in to 1ft effect of the railway as an attractive garden feature in its own right *and* simultaneously the production of a convincing miniature, modelled landscape – and where the two issues are effectively reconciled, rather than working in opposition to each other, as is so often the case at present.

CREATE AN EYESORE

Perhaps we need to take inspiration from the impressionist artists of later periods, most of whom did not attempt to depict landscapes feature by feature, but more effectively went for

Above: The epitome of early 20th Century Narrow Gauge. There is a keen eye behind everything that Laurie Wright does…

Top left: Attention to detail with the track also pays dividends – after all, it sits there permanently, the most obvious indicator of the existence of a railway. When I switched from proprietary to hand-built track, I was stunned by the improvement, not only in 'direct' realism, but also with the effects that the light played with the fully chaired, bull-head rail version. Laurie Wright is, of course, a past master at this, as this immaculately decrepit view shows.

Left: This has to be one of the most realistic photo's I have ever managed to take on a model railway. Laurie Wright has not set out to recreate the Welsh Highland Railway, indeed some of his inspiration derives from nearer to home and the Vale of Rheidol – but this shot could almost be a picture of the real Aberglaslyn Pass near Beddgelert. Every inch of the image shouts Welsh Narrow Gauge, from the weed-infested track, ballast almost top the rail tops, to the dankness of the cutting walls and the spiky but verdant vegetation of the area. Laurie is of course assisted by the fact that his local climate is obligingly prototypical!

Opposite: Another view of Andrew Coward's line, showing the appealing effect of mature vegetation arching over the line.

the broad sweep approach. In this way, we can perhaps mitigate the non-scale vegetation we are using by the simple technique of building banks or backdrops of planting which can then represent stands of trees or bushes within which the shapes of individual plants are lost. This naturally lends itself more to a more naturalistic, shrub-based garden than one comprising formal beds of annuals. Because of the peculiar circumstances in which I built my railway, I have had to think very hard about this issue. The other seven residents of the building did not necessarily want the outside of their building to look like a model village, because such things are clearly not to everyone's taste, and I had to have at least half a thought on the likely impact on others trying to sell their apartments. I also had to think about the effect on my neighbours in other buildings – while I do not set

out to be an unthinking advocate for the crushing uniformity of 'respectable good taste', it was only fair to consider the impact on our part of the street as a whole; I certainly did not want to create an eyesore in the name of my hobby – hence no baseboards on posts!

THE FOCAL POINT

My wife also wished to have some input into the planting side of the scheme – after all, this small and gravelly desert is the only ground we 'own', and we were fortunate that the other residents were content to leave us to our own devices with it. With the third stage of the railway in particular, I planned the whole thing simultaneously from a garden and a railway point

of view. As this part of the plot is along the street frontage, and the knowledge that the locals liked the trains meant that it was also planned with the element of theatre in mind, as discussed previously. To screen the brick wall at the rear, and to hide the fact that there are two lines of track just six feet apart, we planted some *peiris* and *lavenders* in front of the rear track; this will partly obscure trains climbing that part of the line, and serve as a green backdrop for the station towards the front. This passing station was positioned so as to be the focal point of the section, where trains could wait, pass, and be examined by interested passers-by. After climbing the gradient, the trains burst from the greenery to cross a large bridge and round a curve on a rock ledge at prime viewing height, before turning away up the side of the building. The planting has been done in close 'drifts' so that individual plants are not especially distinct, though we did choose them partly on their small leaf size and relatively compact size. We also tried to select a variety of textures to make interesting compositions, and to maintain a reasonably coherent colour scheme – in this case whites, blues and purples – colours that retreat from view and are perhaps more natura-listic than lots of bright primary colours. The only exception to this was the choice of a couple of brightly coloured *azaleas* which, in May suggest the colours of rhododendrons of the Welsh countryside.

Nearer the railway track itself, we used many alpines and herbs, which are mostly small-leaved and low growing, the many varieties of *thyme* and *camomile* being favourites. These tend to provide ground cover and look in scale with the track, while avoiding the hazard of the voracious 'mind your own business' spreading out of control to neighbouring gardens. They also lend a wonderful aroma to the railway on a warm summer's day – a dimension of railway gardening that deserves more attention than it receives, we feel. We also generally avoided miniature conifers, partly out of personal preference and partly because we feel they are rather overdone and do tend to look too manicured.

REMINISCENT OF WOODLAND FLOWERS

At the other end of the line, we faced different problems, namely almost perpetual shade, although the situation was helped when our neighbours decided to fell the large fir tree that shaded the plot early on in construction. The problem here was simply getting anything to grow at all. The aim was to create a woodland feel to the upper terminus of the line, and this has been achieved using a *dwarf maple*, more *azaleas*, *periwinkles*, and *ornamental ivies*, while the *laurel* planted next to the building in desperation has now grown to obscure the view of the rest of the line and helped to create a delightful cameo of a woodland terminus somewhat reminiscent of Abergynolwyn on the Talyllyn Railway, just outside our bedroom window. Again, a restrained colour scheme of blues and whites was

used, reminiscent of woodland flowers, and the subsequent growth of moss has added to this as the past blight of the large conifer receded.

I am not claiming here to offer some radical new approach to planting – indeed I consider myself to be largely ignorant of anything other than very basic horticultural matters, but I am trying to arrive at something which falls into neither of the two traps presented by conventional gardens when it comes to realistic vegetation.

Some garden railway enthusiasts I have met clearly enjoy gardening as an aspect of their hobby, but my impression is that they are outnumbered quite significantly by those for whom a garden is just a place that creates a lot of unwanted work. Be that as it may, the living dimension is surely one of the greatest assets that we outdoor modellers possess, and it seems a pity not to capitalise on the opportunity to set our trains off within a setting that is pleasing to the senses. Given the restrictions that many of us have on space and inherent character of plot, the choice of plants can go a long way to evoking a specific location, and even in more generic ways, to giving our railway a character of its own. They are also the least contrived way of providing the proscenium that our 'railways as theatre' need – and given the choice between manufacturing an artificial landscape from polystyrene, plaster and dyed lint, or bedding in a few plants and letting them grow, I know which I prefer!

LESS DEVELOPED INFRASTRUCTURE

As if the difficulties of planting were not enough, we also have to consider the basic infrastructure required to achieve a railway-like appearance. Buildings and other structures are potentially even more difficult to integrate sympathetically into a garden, as their very presence will shout 'model village'. While narrow gauge railways perhaps have something of an advantage over their full-sized counterparts, in that they generally had less developed infrastructure, a line devoid of any buildings is going to look incomplete. So the question is how to introduce buildings without their looking silly.

Relatively early in my 16mm career, it became apparent to me that there are very few manufacturers who produced convincing proprietary buildings in this scale. This is partly on account of the sheer size of properly scaled models and partly, I believe, down to a lack of demand – though there are signs that this may be about to change. Most offerings appeared to be very much of the caricatured model village type, often under scale, often far too brightly coloured and more redolent of a cartoon than a real building. I was not too worried by this as I had always considered myself something of a buildings specialist on

Left: This is when the work of producing accurate, proper-scale buildings pays off. The locomotive facilities on the Lower Bryandale Railway are cramped in the extreme, but I like to think I have captured the essential muckiness of such places in a space about four feet by one. The ground texture is real coal dust that was sprinkled thickly onto the mortar bed when wet, and brushed clear of loose material only once it had set.

Right: Another shot of Laurie Wright's line. Laurie has observed and captured well the true feeling of an early 20th Century narrow gauge station – as opposed to the imagined interpretation that one sees far more often.

indoor models, and was looking forward to the challenge of making something really big, using authentic materials. What is more, the kind of buildings required by a narrow gauge railway would be fairly distinctive, if not unique, and I did not want to end up with identikit structures as used by many others. However, it was clear that the production of a suitable alternative was going to be a fairly involved task. The main concerns were durability, as I felt the buildings should stay outside full-time - and achieving authentic finishes and colours.

What took me little longer to figure out was why many garden railways managed to feature at least moderately convincing railway buildings but still seemed to get it very wrong when it came to the wider built environment. I came to the conclusion that it was to do with configuration: most railway enthusiasts have sufficient working knowledge of the function and likely positioning of the principle railway buildings, to be able to achieve a railway-like scene quite easily, but much less attention was apparently being given to the other side of the railway fence, where model-village-land seemed the norm. Those garden models that do feature settlements beyond the railway rarely seem to take their lead from real geography – but instead use them simply as a backdrop for the trains. If a model village is the aim, then there is of course nothing wrong with this approach – but realistic it often isn't.

NON-ENGINEER'S APPROACH

I am interested in modelling the whole railway, not just the trains; of course the main aim is to run trains, but I believe that this is most satisfyingly done in the most convincing surroundings possible, and I want the railway to be a convincing and fascinating entity in its own right, even when there are no trains. In this light, modelling the architecture, permanent way, civil engineering and other accoutrements of a functioning railway

Over/under modelling

WORDS LIKE BALANCE, truth and harmony might perhaps seem to have less application to the practical world of model railways than a manual on *fung shui* – but I think that they are relevant if one is taking an artistic approach to our hobby.

I have previously mentioned the potential for large-scale garden models to approach the 'truth' of the real railway to a much greater degree than indoor models. By virtue of all of the qualities discussed elsewhere, what we are engaged in is not so much a *representation* of a railway as the creation of a real, but very small one. For this reason, perhaps we have a greater need and obligation to treat the relationship between our 'small' reality and its full-sized counterpart with respect. Despite my earlier discussions about dramatic effect, we need to consider carefully the compromises that this can bring about. For example, with indoor railways, the use of low-relief buildings is common practice; given our equally severe space restrictions, we might be tempted to borrow the technique, but I am not at all certain that it works out of doors. Given that the boundaries of our modelling space are more loosely defined that neat baseboard edges, the notion of cutting a building in half seems odd indeed, even if it is then placed up against a wall or other boundary. To my eye, this rings highly untrue. Similarly, an indoor model devoid of human representation looks very empty and sterile, and again we might by extension take the same approach. However, there is again a crucial difference: on an indoor model, nothing but the train moves, *nothing* is more than a representation of real life.

On our models, by contrast, almost *everything* is real, including vegetable forms of life, and it somehow seems very inconsistent then to introduce artificial life forms into this context. The fact that the plants blow in the wind, the weather passes over our models and the diurnal cycle works as real, makes it seem all the more incongruous that our plastic or metal figures remain stiff and motionless throughout, another example of a realism-buster, far more destructive than the omission of such details in the first place. If we *must* have figures, would it not be better at least to bring them in at the end of the day, perhaps to move them around periodically, or better still, only position them for photographs where their lack of animation is not obvious? As

for producing figures that actually look real, well I have yet to see more than one or two...

So much for 'truth' – balance and harmony refer to the relationship that our work has with its surrounding environment. To achieve a pleasing and convincing effect, we need to search for equilibrium with those surroundings, where neither garden nor railway dominates the other. This will differ from place to place, depending on the nature of those surroundings, their scale and their other uses.

Despite my use of the term 'model' throughout this book, it is one that I actually hesitate to use for garden railways, as the comments above will explain. In general, however, we need to beware the twin pitfalls of 'over' and 'under' modelling, which is where the artificiality of our undertaking again rears its ugly head.

By under-modelling, I mean a situation where insufficient convincing railway has been represented, so that the overall impression is not of a three-dimensional picture, but rather a crude or functional piece of garden equipment; the traditional understanding of a garden railway tended to fall into this camp. On the other hand, over-modelling is where the model has gone overboard to provide so many features and so much detail that the effect becomes caricatured or forced, and where the garden ceases to look natural under the onslaught of so much artificial intrusion. This can be compounded by well-meaning attempts to reduce real-life distractions, such as garden fences and other paraphernalia, but which nearly always end up drawing more rather than less attention to the offending items. Better to accept their existence and subtly soften them with planting, or draw the eye elsewhere instead.

The most realistically convincing garden railways that I have seen perform the delicate trick of passing through the narrow 'window' between these twin hazards, and the only real way to achieve this is by trial and error, proceeding cautiously step by step, being prepared to alter preconceived plans or aspirations in the light of that which does, or does not work. Being completely frank with oneself is important – it is all too easy to allow convention or complacency to gloss over things that deep down we know are just plain unsatisfactory. Here again, we can perhaps benefit from the thoughts of others who view our work with more detachment than we can achieve ourselves.

Having sufficient judgment to know when to stop, and what not to put in is important in achieving that perfect balance between railway and surroundings, and is an essential tool of the trade – as every artist knows...

---

are just as important as the rolling stock – and just as enjoyable to work on. The closer they can be to the real thing, the happier I am, and this goes as much for getting point rodding working prototypically or a stone wall looking right as it does for building a new coach or wagon. Anything that shouts 'model' is to be avoided as it will be nothing more than a give-away that shatters the illusion, and in order to avoid that, one needs to look more closely at the prototype. I suspect that my original non-engineer's approach has something to do with this, since my interest does not stop at the railway fence, and the appreciation of the geography and social-economic histories of the prototype railways has become an absorbing interest in its own right.

Perhaps the conventional wisdom is that it is not possible to create authentic landscapes outdoors, but I know that not to be true, and I have seen several highly convincing and atmospheric models that have achieved this sense of place to a far higher degree than my own modest efforts have so far permitted. It is certainly true that this is not a low-effort undertaking, but then I suspect that

most of us didn't really go into this rather specialised branch of railway modelling in order to obtain instant off-the-shelf results.

If your aim is to produce something that feels authentic, there can be no substitute for serious time spent scrutinising photographs of real narrow gauge railways. Those who aim for a freelance approach may not perceive the need for this, but I know for a fact that the creators of some of the finest examples of our craft do precisely that. Over time, one absorbs the detail of the way that things looked, or the ways in which things were done – and this can develop into an intuition for how to go about modelling such scenes. This in turn will greatly assist the production of atmospheric and detailed models – for I believe that it is in these two attributes where lies the success of any model. One will also start to appreciate how much of ordinary life we misperceive – and how difficult it can be to get something apparently mundane and ordinary right without a degree of research. It may be felt that this doesn't really matter very much in the greater scheme of running the railway, but if one subscribes to my earlier premise, then all the little errors of perception quickly add up to a model that lacks credibility.

A Skilful Modeller

One of my greatest delights comes from seeing a new model, whether in reality or in a magazine, and exploring it, revelling in all of the things one sees that have been done 'just right'; equally, the disappointment is great where one finds a model that exhausts one's interest quickly, and where the illusion is shattered by things that could have been done much more convincingly or carefully with a little more thought or observation. This may seem pernickety – or maybe it is just the professionally critical teacher in me talking again – but while one is naturally tolerant and tactful about things that disappoint, what greater compliment can one pay to a skilful modeller than to notice all the effort that has gone into getting the thing right? And in terms of published material, what other reason is there for going into print than to submit one's work for the enjoyment and scrutiny of others?

One of the great timeless wisdoms of model-making is *never* to model another model, for fear of compounding errors of reproduction, and the same could be said for modelling from memory of how one *thinks* things are arranged – the reality is frequently different. A classic example of this is the way model buildings are frequently arranged facing the railway, with a road running between the two. While there definitely were examples of such a configuration, it was more often the case that railways ran along the backs of settlements, and as such one would see not the frontages but the back yards and gardens. This may sound unpromising material for an attractive model, but given appropriate examples, there is no reason why it should not be highly intriguing, with the trains passing *behind* forward-facing buildings, and the viewer being treated to views of those seldom seen areas at the rear of buildings, while the frontages are intriguingly (and conveniently) out of sight. Real buildings in real settlements tend to nucleate around a central point, or else straggle along a road, the pattern varying from place to place. In only a few locations was the settlement pattern fully dispersed, even if one of those was parts of upland Wales, which is of course a very popular inspiration for many models. The tendency to position model buildings as a kind of

display rather than as a real settlement is one of the reasons they so often look unconvincing, and given the space such an approach would take, it may be better to go without altogether.

Another problem is that model buildings tend to be simple boxes, rather than the complex shapes of real buildings, presumably on account of their size and difficulty of manufacture; this is particularly noticeable from the rooflines, which are often the most immediately visible parts of most model buildings. And not only are models rarely configured in realistic groupings but more often than not they sit four-square on perfectly flat, equally-sized plots of land all most unlikely in the undulating and frequently impoverished areas where real NG railways were found.

A Street Scene

I must admit at this point that I have at least decided to follow my own advice of leaving something out rather than doing it badly – and therefore I have not included any non-railway buildings on my current line, because I just do not have the space to do them justice. As with many things, I have decided to 'go with the flow' of what the plot will allow rather than force matters just to fulfil unrealistic ambitions. I would dearly love to model a street scene such as that at Welshpool on the W&LLR, but there simply is not the room, so it will have to wait. However, I did construct a scale, albeit small cottage just to test the point, and to prove some techniques, before selling it on.

From this, I concluded that buildings are best modelled to full size, and if space is limited, better simply to choose small prototypes rather than compromise on overall scale and proportion. It is also better to create buildings to fit the topography available rather than vice versa – which may mean building cottages into hillsides etc. Despite my decision to do without, I remain convinced that there have to be successful ways of integrating model buildings into a garden railway without descending into tweeness.

One approach is probably to consider partly concealing buildings with planting, to give a suggestion of buildings sunk into the countryside rather than plonked on top of it, and to consider that essential aspect, grouping buildings realistically to give a varied by subdued set of rooflines. If those buildings are glimpsed from some distance, possibly with their backs to the viewer, they will generate the essential impression of having been there long before the railway, that they have an independent existence, and are not simply decoration for the passing trains. Where buildings come closer to the line, the relationship between the two should be convincing, and there are some superb and fascinating prototypes to draw on here, such as the configuration of buildings and track around Penrhyn Crossing on the Festiniog Railway and at Corris on the eponymous Railway. If done well, a garden model of either of these could be absolutely stunning.

The Added Attraction

Another problem with such scenery is where one should stop; unlike indoor modellers, we do not have that convenient baseboard edge where things just disappear; I am not convinced that it works well to define such spaces very precisely in a gar-

I firmly believe that beauty should not be only skin-deep – at least in buildings such as locomotive sheds. The realism can and should be carried through to the interior, otherwise you are left staring at an empty shell as soon as the doors open – and what better excuse to set up shots like this, *Linda* seen slumbering in Castle Bryan just after Christmas 2007. Even if you are the only one to see such pictures, it all heightens the experience.

Above, top right: I seem to have acquired a reputation for my antipathy to model figures, probably with good reason. I have yet to be convinced that static, lifeless figures do anything but detract from the scenes we create. However, here is the acid test, for you to make up your own mind, but bear in mind that a still photograph may not be a fair test – the effect is different in real time. With thanks to Gavin Robertshaw for sportingly putting up his figure for me to 'prove' him wrong with... I shall say no more!

Right: Minffordd LBR station building from an angle carefully chosen to avoid any full-size distractions. The planting in the background is about eight feet high; as it mostly belongs to our neighbours and pre-dates the railway, I naturally had to live with it. The plants are not especially small-leaved, but as a background to this photographic exercise, they serve their purpose well enough. Note the restrained use of colour on the building.

den, because they will just become arbitrary lines in what is really a continuous space; better to blur the boundaries between to model and non-model worlds. Yet when you have modelled buildings, one feels one really should model the spaces around them, the roads and paths that give access, and so on, and this creates a whole new dilemma which again threatens to turn the garden into a synthetic-looking model village. If one starts modelling roads, where in turn will these stop? Or should one gradually take over the whole garden in the process? As yet, the methods for depicting such scenic elements out of doors are not very developed, and few of those that I have seen have been particularly convincing. Perhaps it is better to avoid the issue by minimising the need for these features. If buildings are only seen from a distance, through vegetation, or from the rear aspect, the need to portray streets and associated para-phernalia is reduced. This may be a disappointment for those who long to model a street scene with working lamps and the rest – but to do it properly realistically is a challenge I have yet to see completely successfully attempted.

As always, I believe that it is better to leave something out than portray it unconvincingly. If one must have roads on one's model, perhaps it is better to use *bona fide* garden paths as such – they obviously perform a useful function in themselves and given the use of small paving slabs or similar where path and railway coincide, they are not excessively wide to represent a road in 16mm scale. In this way, the route ways so described are less likely to raise any domestic objections, and they are also

less likely to end abruptly after a few feet. One can also have the added attraction of level crossings that traverse functioning rights of way, rather than non-descript ribbons of concrete!

All of this implies having a lot of space to play with, which is something that many of us simply don't have. From my experience, it seems better to have few, high realism, full-scale buildings than a lot of unrealistic, under-scale ones, and to leave the non-railway buildings out altogether if you don't have the room to do them justice. At some point in the future, when I hopefully have more land to play with, I still expect to restrict the non-railway buildings to one or two cameo scenes that I particularly want to recreate, rather than attempting to create a complete model landscape which, even apart from the huge amount of work involved, I believe is almost inevitably doomed to end up looking like toy-town.

THE ISSUE OF LIGHTING

Another problematic issue with model buildings out of doors is how to make them blend into their surroundings in the way that most established real ones do, and the other key consideration here is colouring. Indoor railway modellers have begun to take the issue of lighting seriously, since it can make a dramatic difference to the believability of the scene being created, and I think this is at least as much of an issue for us outdoor types. For a start, we can use the one type of lighting that indoor modellers can only dream of – natural light. The significance of this should not be underestimated; without wishing to embark on a technical discourse on the science of colour temperatures, suffice it to say that daylight is far stronger than even the most powerful artificial light source, and it can play havoc with the colours you thought you were producing when creating a model indoors. What is more, unlike an indoor model, our lighting conditions are neither controllable nor constant, though in terms of realism, the latter is actually a boon rather than a problem if used correctly. That said, incorrect use of colour is a very quick way to spoil an otherwise convincing model. Since garish colours will cause a model to stand out blatantly against the natural surroundings, this is also a direct route to convincing others that the railway detracts from the garden rather than enhances it – unless they also happen to be into whimsy too!

In general terms, the impact of daylight over artificial light will be to wash colours out – shades that looked dark or substantial indoor will normally look less so outside. Despite that, or perhaps because of it, many garden models seem to be far too strongly coloured – though whether that is through the slightly surreal intentions of some modellers, or simple failure to check with consequent over-compensation, is debatable. Again, I come back to emulating the prototype as the surest way to avoid problems. In the case of human structures, this isn't too difficult as paint finishes can be easily replicated. What is more difficult is replicating natural finishes, and this is an area of garden modelling which is still developing quite rapidly, and where there is as yet no real established methodology.

Many commercial buildings are produced from resin, which has the main advantage of being virtually weatherproof, and can replicate detail quite sharply if well done. The main drawback from a colour point of view is that it needs painting, and given the material, there are few alternatives to doing this. Being synthetic, it is also going to weather very differently from the materials it purports to represent. Other commercial models have been produced in plastic or ceramic, both of which offer benefits, but neither of which performs like the real materials. There is also, to my mind, an inherent problem with using a single material to portray the multiple materials from which most buildings are made. Perhaps the greatest difficulty is in modelling masonry, whether stone or brick. Commercially made buildings normally need to be painted, but paint never reproduces stone or brick finishes fully convincingly.

ATMOSPHERIC AND CHARACTERFUL

Often, the colour is far too intense, and far too uniform, and the texture of the real material is almost entirely lacking – and

these things matter more in the large scales than they might in, say N gauge. Frequently one sees model buildings where individual stones have been picked out in a different colour in the name of realism – but when was the last time you saw a building that looked so regularly and strongly bi-tonal? If one *has* to use paint in this way, it is essential to use a very limited colour range, so that variation is restricted to small differences, and the only real way to achieve a convincingly random effect is to paint each stone separately – not a job for those short of patience! What limited experimentation I have done on this suggests that much-diluted colour wash is going to achieve a more convincing effect – though it is essential to check out of doors that the colour will not simply 'disappear'. This approach also reduces the risk of clogging any surface texture that the base material has. It seems better to me to consider the end effect during the construction stage. For a start, the closer one can come to real materials, the better the result will be. Hence I model wood with wood, metal with metal and increasingly, stone with stone. The accompanying panel offers more detail on the techniques I have used for my buildings to date.

Making realistic buildings in any scale is a time-consuming process, but it can be fascinating in its own right – and doubly so in the large scales because of the impressive bulk of the end result, and the scope for extending realism into the materials and constructional processes as well as the final visual effect. Careful consideration of this aspect is needed if we are to achieve credible results which will blend with and enhance the garden rather than detracting from it. Creating an atmospheric and characterful railway depends at least as much on getting these issues right as on the trains themselves – and all the more so if we are working with severe constraints on space. At such times, it may seem wasteful to devote space to the luxury of 'scenery' rather than track and trains, but I believe this is another of those situations where a little counter-intuitive thinking will go a long way towards creating a believable and appealing model rather than something bland; seen this way, the investment of space and time in a few good quality buildings pays a handsome dividend.

A great attraction of working out of doors is that our models are subject to the diurnal cycle. While some indoor modellers have added varied lighting effects to their models, we have the real thing! The logical conclusion is to add lighting, and the experience of running the trains at dusk or even after dark can be quite enchanting. Quite apart from the practical work involved in doing this, it is another aspect that needs to be done sensitively and with restraint, for the results of doing it

Left: One of the joys of large-scale modelling is the satisfying size of even small details. This weather vane was fretted from brass scraps and has graced the top of Castle Bryan locomotive shed for the past two years. It was a joy to make, and has sufficient weight to function very well.

Opposite: I can almost hear some readers murmuring about the deceptive effects of the carefully chosen pictures in this book. Well, I don't make any apologies for that. Photography is becoming more and more an integral part of what we do, and it presents perhaps the ultimate opportunity for realism in large scale modelling. The only real 'principle' used here has been to take pictures from near ground level – no manipulation has been employed at all, and the vast majority of the pictures were taken on nothing more sophisticated than an Olympus compact digital. However, it is of course important that our railways should look good from more normal viewpoints, so I include these two views of the ever-magnificent Tarren Hendre to show that careful scenic work looks appealing from whatever viewpoint. Photos: Andrew Crookell

badly are literally glaring! Again, it depends on what effect you are after, but to do lighting realistically raises a whole host of new problems. To begin with, there are issues of access to bulbs, and while it is easy enough to upend a building, this in itself creates a difficulty since buildings that leak light around their ground line destroy more illusions than they create. It may be better to seal the walls to the ground and have removable roofs – so long as the roofs still sit properly on the buildings, don't blow away in strong winds, and the eaves can be equally light-proofed. On my most recent buildings, I have inserted brass tubes, which protrude below the walls at an inconspicuous point, and then curve up inside the building to a height at which the light source will sit. These are painted black to remove issues of reflections, and then a grain of wheat bulb is pushed up the tube until it just protrudes at the top. Bulbs can then be changed relatively easily when needed without having to unearth the building at all.

LONGEVITY OF LIGHT SOURCE

Talk of bulbs leads me to consider the light source itself; the use of LED's is gaining in popularity thanks to their longevity, but I have yet to see one that creates just the right warm glow that we are mostly after; whites are far too blue, while yellows look like sodium street-lighting. The lack of an element in LED's also seems to make them cast a strangely directionless, two-dimensional light. Bearing in mind that we may well be trying to replicate gas lighting, that colour temperature is all-important, and even on purely aesthetic grounds, cold colours do not really achieve a pleasant effect. It is worth remembering that buildings do not tend to have all of their lights on simultaneously, so it may be better just to light a few rooms than have all rooms in all buildings blazing, while diming the intensity of the source will both be

more realistic and prolong bulb life. When it comes to street-lights, the same issues apply – and remember that with some gas lights it should be almost possible to see the filament of the bulb in order to achieve a realistic effect. All of the foregoing also applies to rolling stock – and why would one light buildings if the trains are to run in the dark? However I have yet to resolve the issues of accessing bulbs for maintenance while also concealing wiring satisfactorily in coaches where the lights will de facto show up shortcuts. Moreover, the issues of leaking light are at least as problematic with rolling stock as with buildings. I am however greatly attracted to the head and tail lamps now available, powered with watch batteries – though longevity of light source is currently so limited as to be frustrating, the effect is pure magic – especially when one is removes from the train and placed still glowing on a platform while one runs the locomotive round!

It is when considering matters like those in this chapter that the full, enormous implications of undertaking a garden railway become obvious. Even a small model can entail a huge amount of work to get right all of the aspects necessary to create a convincing model – and it is understandable that most workers, especially those whose interest inclines more specifically towards the trains, perhaps haven't really bothered to explore these avenues fully.

Many may well be prepared to live without them, but for my money, it is in these very things that lie both the peculiar magic of garden railways, and the challenge that I personally seek. While their specific omission may not always be immediately obvious, the consequence may be in the overall level of 'payback' of the resultant models; I return to my initial thesis that high quality work in any discipline is well worth it, in terms of satisfaction derived and personal 'growth' achieved – but it is not achieved without a commensurate price being paid!

Building constructional techniques

To DATE I HAVE MADE all of my buildings from a shell of glued/screwed exterior grade plywood; though durability is an issue, some of mine have been outside for three years with no attention at all. This of course this is still relatively short and only time will tell how long they actually stand up – and whether the consequences of their not doing will be sufficient to make me change tack as my handiwork gradually disintegrates! I hope that the precautions I have used will give the buildings sufficient life to be useful, and that they will be capable of repair when necessary – after all, what real building is expected to withstand the weather indefinitely without maintenance in the way that we seem to expect our models to do?

All of the basic shells are treated inside with wood preservative, and the lower edges sealed either with extruded PVC 'L' section, aluminium strip or silicone sealer, as happens to be appropriate or to hand. Paint finishes are either masonry paint or oil-based enamels, diluted a little if necessary, and applied over a car-primer base coat. These are both hardwearing, but in due course, the buildings will need a repaint – just like the real thing. If one fixes the building down with silicone sealer, it is fairly easy to cut it free for maintenance. The ply carcase is overlaid with lime wood or similar sheet, cut into individual planks where required, and glued in place with a generous coat of weatherproof PVA glue. Doors usually utilise the underlying ply to achieve the required depth and weatherproof-ness (no gaps round the edges), with frames built up from strip wood. Window frames are similarly done – but after installing panes cut from 2mm picture frame glass. Nothing else brings a building to life quite as well as convincing windows – and nothing quite has the reflective properties of real glass. It is not hugely expensive; it can be marked with an overhead projector pen and fairly easily cut using a wheeled cutter obtainable from any glazier. My local glazier was quite happy to give me a quick lesson in cutting – the key technique is never to scribe more than one line, and then to snap the cut over a closely supported strip of thin wood – one millimetre is plenty. It is of course essential to remember just how sharp fragments of glass can be, to wear suitable eye protection and to dispose of all splinters immediately and carefully. With practice, it is possible to cut close-fitting windows that need minimal fixing in place – for which I normally use a smear of two-part epoxy resin. Window frames are then built up directly on the glass using more strip wood secured with epoxy; the methodical will paint the strips first – but I find that a steady hand normally suffices, and glass will in any case allow you to clean up any errors with a scalpel once dry without the risk of scratches.

DISTINCTLY OUT OF PLACE

Metal is normally needed for gutters, strap hinges etc, and is best primed before painting. Brass is the easiest metal to work – aluminium is too soft. There are some occasions where I do resort to plastic where no brass section is available. Doorknobs and the like, can be turned from strip wood in a mini drill held

Opposite: Bill Winter has been using real stone for his entire buildings, and I think you will agree that the effect is stunning; I am intending to follow his example in future. What is more, they will weather like the original, too. Note the clutter lying around – nicely judged, with just enough to achieve the effect, but still restrained in its execution.

Above: Realistic and well made buildings contribute a significant amount to the overall character of a railway, and can do a lot do diminish distractions in the unmodelled background. This station building by Jeremy Ledger is an absolute gem. Notice the sagging roof, modelled by creating sagging 'rafters' inside, before adding real slates, the rotting timber and the suitably dim lamp. One hardly notices the garden wall in the background.

Right: The corrugated iron roof on this goods shed was achieved using take-away containers from my local Indian restaurant. These were opened out; then crimped using a device for crimping cardboard, bought at an art shop. The sheet was cut into panels, laid overlapping and secured with impact adhesive, and then spray-painted.

horizontally in a drill frame and used as a lathe with cutting mostly done with needle files. When colouring wood or metal surfaces, it is again important to remember basic colour theory – and indeed history. Colour intensities will change out of doors, so it is important to experiment, remembering that not only will bright, primary colours end up looking very toy-like, but also that historically, bright colours were difficult and expensive to produce, and so the colour range was restricted and dull compared to what we see today. Greens, browns, creams, greys pale blues and rusty reds seems to work fairly well,

whereas bright reds, blues and greens – and pure black and white – look distinctly out of place to my eye. Gloss paint will exacerbate this situation, since it does not scale well; matt is a better bet, or satin if a new-look finish is required. A useful tip gleaned from Andrew Coward is never to use pure black or white – they just look too intense and pristine – very dark and very pale greys respectively are always more convincing, whether on a building or an item of rolling stock.

The biggest headache remains the masonry. So far, I have used a thick skin of exterior grade filler – a good quality one, as

Left: This is one of my earlier efforts, made while I was still refining my techniques. It follows the same basic structure as detailed later. The roof is made from strips of black plasticard, half-cut, overlapped and sanded with the slope to dull the plastic and achieve a slate-like texture.

Lower: Especially with 'open' buildings, it is worth modelling interior structures – and this can be satisfying in its own right. These trusses were made up from softwood strip on a simple pin-jig, and then stuck to the underside of the roof, before the connecting timbers were added.

Opposite: The pay-back comes in a picture like this, with the stained trusses adding plausibility to a scene that would look unrealistically empty without them.

the cheaper varieties contain a higher percentage of sand and crumble more easily. This is a messy job, since it involves covering the whole building in one go, so as to avoid weaknesses along drying lines between adjacent applications. Other weak points are at the corners of buildings, where the filler is likely to thin; I avoid this by putting a 45° flat onto the corner and sticking on a small fin of about 2mm strip wood, which holds the filler, much on the same way that a plasterer would use a corner strip to achieve a true corner. I make a filler mix quite wet, and smear the carcase with a thin layer of weatherproof PVA adhesive; the theory is that one or the other will encourage the filler to bond strongly to the wood – and it seems to work. So far, I have only once coloured the filler mix, this being done to represent brick work, and I used artists' watercolour tubes, employing quite a dense colour as it will pale significantly when dry. Trial and error is the best way to find what works, but it is important to limit the amount of paint added, as it will weaken the filler if the content becomes too high. Pre-colouring worked better than surface painting, and the inconsistencies in mixing the paint provided some natural variation. It was possible to add

some highlights using a dry brushing technique later, and in this instance I finished it with a matt varnish as an extra coating for weather protection. For stonework, however, I have always left the filler uncoloured, though this can produce results that are a little pale and uniform, though of a very good texture; natural weathering has generally added contrast and depth all by itself, given time.

TRIAL AND ERROR

There are many ways to produce a stone or brick pattern. They can be laboriously scribed when the filler is dry, though this both blunts tools very quickly, and produces huge amounts of unpleasant dust. Another quicker but more difficult technique is to scribe when the filler is 'green' or very nearly dry. It requires practice to achieve a convincing pattern and mistakes are not easily rectified. Most recently, I have used stamp blocks built up using strips of thirty thou Plastikard on end, in a kind of honeycomb effect, which was then used to indent the filler again when green. Trial and error is needed here, as the cutter will pull a lot of the filler away if applied too early, but will not make an impression if it is too dry. It is possible to make up such stamps on top of printouts of photos of real stonework, so that the pattern is highly realistic, and the stamp can be used inverted and reversed in order to vary the pattern, if desired. I normally use a simple edge of Plastikard to scribe corner stones, lintels etc. first, then I use fillets of filler to add window sills to the wet filler, working it almost like clay, before stamping the surface, keeping horizontal courses consistent where necessary, and using the simple edge to join individual stamp patterns into an overall finish.

The above method can achieve controllable and realistic results, and I have used it to represent both stone and brick, though the latter needs care because of the small size of the blocks involved. However, as time has progressed, I have concluded that there is no substitute for using the original material, and I will probably do so more and more in future though the thought of constructing a large building entirely from cut slate

Top left: Stonework being added using exterior filler. The cutter used to stamp the stonework patter is visible in the foreground.

Above: The cottage taking shape, with the stonework dry, and real glass added in the windows.

Centre top: Timber buildings can be made on a similar shell. This is the station building for my new passing station, based closely on Tan-y-bwlch on the Festiniog Railway. The timber is overlaid using lime or similar sheet and strip. Using weatherproof pva is essential!

Centre lower: The chimney was made up as per the stonework on the earlier cottage, but pre-coloured using artists' watercolour tubes.

Lower: Part of the finished building; the roof was covered with real slate, and the valleys lined with real lead from a dolls house supplier; material fidelity cannot be bettered. Details such as gutters, timetable and the clock all add to the character of the end product.

is daunting to say the least; time will tell! Workers such as Laurie Wright and Bill Winter have shown that it is perfectly possible to use real stone for models, and I have done the same for retaining walls and such like. This is a laborious process, but the end result is worth it in terms of successfully blending buildings into their settings and achieving finishes close to real buildings. It is possible to cut old roof slates on a wet-wheel tile cutter, though it is a messy and noisy job, and should come with a health warning – slate dust is respirable, therefore a potentially dangerous material, and due precautions should be taken to avoid inhaling it.

USED REAL SLATES

Roofs are extremely important in achieving realism, as they tend to be the most visible part of any model building, and so are worth doing properly. I have used overlapping strips of half-cut Plastikard slates, before sanding to dull them and provide texture, but more recently I have again used real slates, and these can be obtained from dolls house suppliers. They may be a little thick for our purposes, but they are incomparable in appearance, and can even be augmented with real lead flashing etc. They also add a great deal to the weatherproofing of the building.

I have gone into some constructional detail with this section as I believe it is one of the areas where much needs to be done in terms of creating realistic settings for our models, but where there is also a huge gain to be had from aiming high.

IF A MODEL RAILWAY IS A PIECE OF THEATRE, it's pretty obvious who the actors are. No matter how interesting the railway, the stars are undoubtedly the trains themselves, and yet, despite the attention that many modellers give them, they can still one of the most problematic things to get right.

I have never worked out exactly what it is about railway engines, and steam locomotives in particular that garners people's fascination in the way that they do; perhaps it harks back to a primitive empathy with large lumbering beasts and the tracks that they leave. It has been said many times that a steam locomotive in particular is the nearest thing to a living creature that man has yet made, and this is no less so with our small steam engines. In fact, this is the greatest asset for realism that we have – the fact that when you oil, fuel and water a garden-scale steam locomotive, light the fire and let it come alive, it hits just about all of the same 'buttons' as the real thing: it sounds right, it even smells right, and it brings the railway alive as no electric model is able to do. And yet narrow gauge models somehow fall at the last hurdle when it comes to total realism; while many Gauge 1 standard gauge models look absolutely right at the head of a train, even if the lines they are running on are pretty rudimentary, until now narrow gauge trains still retain something that says (expensive) toy about them.

ENTRY-LEVEL MODELS

The reasons for this are probably many, though affordability has to be one of them – narrow gauge models are usually regarded as the cheaper end of the live steam market, and as such compromises have been made with their manufacture on commercial grounds. Equally, they are seen as the novice's way into live steam, and that combination of cost constraints and supposed lack of discernment on the part of the market has perhaps allowed manufacturers to get away with fairly basic, generic models for some time; the more demanding modeller had to go to one of the various cottage industries and pay considerably more to obtain a fine narrow gauge model. This now seems to be changing, as the principal players in the market are raising their game, providing increasing levels of detail and producing locomotives at least based on prototypes – even if they are still taking some pretty large liberties with them in the name of commercial viability. In recent years, water level gauges and boiler refill systems have become more or less standard, and who knows where things will be in even another five years? From my limited experience, the development of a lubricator top-up system and properly functioning water tanks would be at the top of my own wish list. At the same time, of course, prices have risen to cover these extras, though the parallel development of entry-level models has compensated to some extent.

POLISHED BRASSWORK

Yet, as I said, despite the increasing mechanical sophistication, many locomotives still look like toys. Perhaps it is the use of gas firing, which is much cleaner than coal; many coal-fired models

In the last few years, the locomotives being offered by companies such as Roundhouse and Accucraft have seen massive strides in realism. This single Fairlie is light-years ahead of models of just a few years ago. Detailed castings and developments such as inside valve gear and boiler-fill systems have improved both the aesthetic and technical effect of our star performers. Photo: Tag Gorton

Opposite: There is still quite a lot that can be done by even a non-engineer like me to take things a stage further. Perhaps the single biggest advance is to be had by lining the locomotive out. Compare these pictures of *Linda* wearing factory-finish unlined black at the LBR 2008 open day and the same locomotive after I finally summoned up the courage to line her out using a Peter Spoerer lining pen. I do wish we could be given at least the choice of a satin paint finish over high gloss, though. Photo: Sara Stock (top), Ian Stock (lower)

Right: Neil Ramsay make the most wonderful models of Irish three-foot gauge rolling stock. This is a Lough Swilly fish van and a classic example of capitalising on large scale modelling rather than denying it. The doors are fully functional, and the inside can be revealed to be complete with fish boxes. Photo: Neil Ramsay

Centre: Another example of Neil's work, again showing the delicacy of detail obtainable, and yes, these are hard-working models which run regularly on Neil's railway, not stuffed specimens for the display case. This is an NCC goods van. Photo: Neil Ramsay

Lower: Another shot of rolling stock under construction, in this case the WLLR brake van. This is a wonderfully therapeutic aspect of our hobby, requiring only time to achieve a pleasing effect.

seem to acquire a much more authentic layer of grime! Some manufacturers still paint their models to a high gloss finish, and while these models undoubtedly look superb when displayed on a sales stand, that finish is just too 'high' to be realistic. Similarly, too much polished brasswork has often featured on freelance models, though the move towards prototype models seems to be dealing with this. And finally, the fact that many locomotives come with fairly rudimentary colour schemes and devoid of any lining does detract from their realism and true splendour.

There has been a lot of debate about these issues on the various internet discussion groups, and it is far from clear how such issues can be moved forward. For many, the rudimentary appearance of the locomotives is not important compared with the chance for hands-on running experience with a real steam locomotive, so perhaps the demand has simply not been there for more detail. There has also been the claim that fine detail is not compatible with garden models as it is too fragile – though this does not seem to be an outlook shared by the gauge 1 fraternity.

From the perspective of this book, the key issue is how to achieve a high degree of realism with our trains, and there is little point in starting from other than where we are. I for one have no engineering experience or facilities to allow me to make my own locomotives, and if I am honest, not the interest, either. I suspect that many of those coming from an indoor model background are similar, and the general decline in people's practical ability and facilities means that increasingly locomotives will be brought rather than made. A consideration is, however, the choice of motive power. For many, myself included, one of the main factors in the move outdoors was the opportunity to run live steam – but as we have seen, it does have its drawbacks.

FUNCTIONING MODEL DIESELS

The problem is that any of the alternatives move us away from authenticity and back towards the world of 'simulated' loco-motives of the indoor scales. This is a 'live' issue for me – I started out with a determination that the LBR would be solely steam operated, and so, thus far, it has remained. However, the tempta-tion of the instant availability of other forms of motive power has

not been absent, and I am considering how a suitably vintage-type of diesel might be produced. The problem, though, is still one of fidelity – while functioning model diesels have been made in 16mm scale, so far I have yet to hear one that sounds anything much like the real thing – or that is acceptably quiet for my surroundings. As track power is neither viable nor desirable on my line, this leaves only battery power as a more viable proposition; at least the locomotive remains literally that – self-moving – even if we have lost the 'truth' of real steam power. The addition of a sound card can offset the auditory deficit to a considerable extent – and perhaps we should be looking for working exhaust elements to push us some of the way back towards steam-equivalence. That said, I find myself increasingly

swayed by those who favour the ready availability of radio-controlled battery power that, with its controllability, is superior even to the steam locomotives.

One of the psychological problems that also hold us back is the rather intimidating level of capital expenditure involved in our locomotives; having spent perhaps a four-figure sum on a new model, there is a big mental barrier to overcome in meddling with it, and it took me quite some time to beat this. This is not the place to discuss the techniques for upgrading locomotives, and others have written about it far more knowledgably than I could, but it is evident that there are cosmetic changes that can make a big difference. The gloss paint can be toned down somewhat with a coat of satin varnish, while adding real coal to bunkers and glazing to spectacle plates makes more difference than one might expect. Lining out the locomotive makes a staggering improvement; while this can be costly to have done professionally – and understandably many want a professional job – I summoned up the nerve to have a go using a lining pen and was able to produce a quite satisfactory job with a couple of days' experience and practice. Very often, the fear of having a go at the perceived 'black arts' (such as locomotive lining), is greater than the technical difficulty of actually doing it!

Some people, such as Andrew Coward, go further and weather their locomotives, achieving superb results, although there is a school of thought that says 'real' locomotives should just be allowed to weather naturally. Having seen Andrew's results, there is no doubt in my mind that effective weathering can turn a straightforward commercial model into something much more realistic, though I have yet to do the same to my own locomotives. One issue with all such paint-related matters is to

Andrew Coward achieves excellent effects by weathering his rolling stock. These wagons are mostly standard Accucraft Lynton & Barnstaple stock, but he has repainted them into his line's house colours, and then weathered them until you really would not spot their origins.

ensure that the surface to be worked on is clean and completely grease-free, more of an issue with steam-powered models than electric ones, especially if one is doing such jobs retrospectively, after a locomotive has been running for some time.

USE AUTHENTIC MATERIALS

Realistic rolling stock presents one with rather more possibilities. The growing availability of high-quality ready-to-run models is undoubtedly a boon for those whose interest does not lie in rolling stock – they are well detailed and robust, and not always expensive. However, as with indoor modelling, the risk now exists of finding identikit trains all over the place. On the other hand, while there are many respectably well-detailed kits on the market, it seems as if many garden modellers are content to run semi-scale representations of trains as their main attention is elsewhere, and the majority of models seem built firstly and only for strength rather than the atmosphere and realism that can be bestowed by adding rather more detail. As with buildings, the opportunity to use authentic materials was an important priority when considering rolling stock; I wanted to capture that complex pattern of a panelled coach side, the particular shine of brass grab handles and the very 'woody' nature of

This picture of a train crossing the original Glen Olibhe Viaduct on the earlier incarnation of the LBR shows the relative impact of locomotive and stock. The locomotive is a bog standard freelance 'Lady Anne' from Roundhouse, the rolling stock all either scratchbuilt or detailed kits. The overall effect is more convincing than such a locomotive might be if seen on its own.

some of the really quite primitive goods stock found on narrow gauge railways. I was extremely fortunate to meet Neil Ramsay fairly early on in my outdoor modelling career. He builds exquisite models of Irish three-foot gauge prototypes and I learned a huge amount from him about building rolling stock from multiple layers of thin birch ply. Given the kind of skills and patience that an indoor modeller would fairly routinely deploy, it is possible to build rolling stock that captures the real essence of narrow gauge trains, and looks fully the part disappearing up the line. I have found that building rolling stock has almost become a hobby in its own right, and eminently suitable for those times or seasons when outdoor running is not possible. The research required to build an accurate model and the subsequent con-struction process really are very rewarding and not least means that you can build up an atmospheric and highly individual rake at relatively little expense. Given how much effort goes into the locomotives, I find it surprising that the rolling stock to run behind them seems to have been such a neglected topic. What is more, given that a locomotive may account for 20% or less of the total length of a train, well-modelled rolling stock can go a long way towards lifting the overall impact, and compensating for any deficiencies on the locomotive itself.

So, despite the limitations discussed above, it is possible today to produce a train that, while not millimetre-accurate, does provide the atmosphere of the real thing, and sitting there, gently hissing at the head of a train, the locomotives do look rather splendid. However, there are other aspects to realism that also need consideration, the way in which the models move being one of the more obvious. Despite the mass of live steam models, they still function using the physics of the full-sized world and as such it is quite difficult to persuade them to move in a consistently realistic way. Starting and stopping are particular headaches, while it is also quite difficult to persuade them to move at something approaching a scale speed when the boiler pressure is trying to send the thing into orbit. The technicalities of how such things might be ironed out are beyond the scope of this book, but the advent of radio control has played a major part in improving the realism with which our trains move, albeit at the expense of reducing the hands-on 'driver input' with the locomotive. And yet, one sees many radio controlled models being driven at speeds more appropriate for a modern express than the ten or fifteen mph of the average real narrow gauge train. Scale speed is notoriously difficult to gauge, but as Paul Sherwood has observed, filming our trains from the line side and watching the playback will reveal that more likely than not what we thought was a scale speed is way too fast. Perhaps it is too much to expect absolute adherence to real life here – the trains would move intolerably slowly for many, but one that is moving far too fast will always destroy that illusion that we seek to create. It is as if the lead actor came onto the stage, garbled his lines and left at the first opportunity, before we have had a chance to appreciate the performance.

COMPLETELY RAILWAY-LIKE

Radio control coupled with boiler top-up systems should in theory make it much more possible for us to cover the whole range of manoeuvres observed on a real railway, and yet the majority of running still seems to be of the round-and-round type, perhaps with a few pieces of rolling stock in tow but perhaps not. I think

this stems from the sheer undeniable pleasure of running a garden train and watching it in motion – and it is often compounded by the fact that the line is not at a convenient height for more complex movements. What is more, in the back of one's mind is the niggling awareness that unlike an electric model, one has a relatively limited running time before needing to stop and refuel. I must admit that I am as guilty as anyone on this front, and yet I feel that simply shuttling back and forth with the same train (given my lack of continuous run) neither feels completely railway-like nor is it making the most of the operational possibilities that exist. One may well ask what the point is of hair shirt wearing in one's hobby, but as with other aspects, there is perhaps a solution that will retain the pleasurable benefits of the easy approach with the improvement of something more realistic.

The easiest thing to do, and yet one that is widely ignored, is to create longer intervals between trains. On an end to end run, making the run-round procedure more relaxed immediately increases the realism and not only does it look better, it *feels* better too. Then the train should stand at the station for a suitable length of time before departing; the 'wasted' steam is an issue here, but I have found that it is more a state of mind than a practical problem on a short line – more tricky is overcoming the quite powerful urge to set off as soon as possible, though

Every railway needs a source of traffic, and Nant Gorris quarry on the Maesffordd & Nant Gorris line is a fine example. Paul Sherwood has even gone so far as to create an underground adit into which quarry loco's may push and pull wagons. An alternative might be to borrow from indoor railway practice by arranging such a feature to pass into a concealed siding, perhaps in a shed, where loads may be added.

it *is* possible to train yourself out of this! In fact, the sight of a locomotive sitting quietly hissing in at the platform can be a pleasure in its own right, and one can even get on with a few station or line side duties in the meantime. For the price of a small extra hassle, the use of functioning head and tail lamps, and vacuum pipes means there are more of those duties to be done at the ends of the line, and this can be developed further for example through the creation of functioning point lever frames, so that you can play signalman as well. It is surprising how many modellers do not actually seem to bother using their stations at all; while at a terminus one has no choice, given that most lines are continuous, I have observed in my time very few station stops – let alone convincingly long ones.

The next enhancement one can make is to undertake some rudimentary shunting; the most necessary manoeuvre is that

Right: This County Donegal Railways coach demonstrates why such rolling stock can take over 200 hours to construct; this is almost a hobby in its own right. Just look at the detail of that interior! However, you can still obtain good results with rather less time committed, and as their construction methods and materials are closely related to the original, they will always achieve an individuality of appearance that even the best mass-produced commercial models will struggle to acquire.
Photo: Neil Ramsay

Lower: Thankfully, a large number of original vehicles still exist in the preservation era, and some have been restored to their full early appearance. Pictures like this of an NWNGR coach at Caernarfon on the reopened Welsh Highland Railway are invaluable as modelling aids. There are also many drawings available from sources such as the 7mm Narrow gauge Modellers' Society, which can be easily re-scaled by scanning on a computer.

required to compose a suitable train, rather than relying on sky-hooks. While passenger trains often ran as fixed sets, on goods trains, brake vans may well need to be shunted to the other end before departure, and if picking up or dropping off wagons, one should pay at least some attention to train composition; under normal circumstances, perishables and livestock ran at the head of the train, and where appropriate, fitted or through-piped vehicles had to be at the front. For more on such matters, I can do no better than recommend Bob Essery's book, which while dealing with the standard gauge, is excellent for developing one's understanding of the complexity of real railway operational issues.

STEAM GRADUALLY DRIFTING

As part of this drive for realistic operation, I normally set the line out for a running session with various vehicles distributed at different points; not only does this provide a better visual setting than single-train operation (whenever did you see a real railway with no rolling stock parked in sidings?) but it also provides the opportunity to pick up and drop off vehicles as the mood takes me. I also raise steam in the locomotive shed area rather than at a random point on the line – and the ritual starts with the opening of the loco shed doors, silly perhaps, given that motive power does not actually live inside, but it all adds to the feel. I often put out more locomotives than the ones I will be using, to give the shed a more lived-in feel. I prepare the loco, and then sometimes push it inside the shed to heat up, steam gradually drifting out of the shed's clerestory roof, at which point we can back out and go off shed in the proper manner, in search of a train.

In the peculiar setting of my own line, I have also increasingly taken account of the way in which others see the trains. Much of this was done at the planning and building stages – for example, I took particular care to ensure that the trains *sounded* right when passing over the bridges. When operating, I try to ensure that station stops are authentically long – while getting this wrong can lead to impatience (especially with my younger audiences), building a little anticipation can be a good thing. Locomotives with whistles are a bonus here, though my own have none –

but as so often, getting it right is important, since a whistle that sounds wrong is perhaps worse than none at all. Thanks to my particular situation, I also have the amusing little trick that can be played with a little practice, which is to remain completely out of sight as the train passes along the main street-side section – and which can produce some interesting reactions from those who are either not expecting it, or who have not seen it before! When playing to a wider audience, the degree of driver intrusion in the scene may be worth bearing in mind.

Despite all of the foregoing, running the railway becomes many times more rewarding when one is not doing it alone. The sociability of the garden railway scene bears great testament to the enjoyment of sharing this hobby. It is very difficult to control more than one live steam locomotive at once – and it perhaps detracts from the driving experience to do so – so for a more complex operation, one needs other people. On my small line, the optimum is probably two trains, though we have had as many as four running at once, at which point it becomes too much like one of those shunting puzzles and for me loses a lot of realism. With two drivers, the attraction of single track becomes real – one needs to wait at a passing point until the line is clear – and the experience of that wait, followed by the appearance of the oncoming train chuntering into the adjacent

When I started out, I was determined that the LBR was to be exclusively steam-worked. However, with the passage of the years, the attractions of having some instant movement became more apparent, especially at the end of the day when time and light is short. The problem was that the Welsh Narrow Gauge lines did not ever really develop anything suitable for my requirements. In particular, I wanted something that would not need a run-round at each end in the failing light, and that meant a railcar. The answer was to invent my own prototype, and the result was this Drewry railcar, based on those that ran on the West Clare and Weston, Clevedon & Portishead Railways. Apparently, Col. Stephens did consider something like it for the Welsh Highland, so this might-have-been is hopefully not too wide of the mark. I also wanted to see whether such a vehicle could be made to sit comfortably with more prototype-derived vehicles; on that front, I am reasonably happy. It is seen here not quite complete, on test at Queen's Forest Road.

Here's another view of Bill Winter's wonderful station building at Bachwen the Llyfni Vale Railway. Yet more evidence that doing it the 'real' way has no equal. I love the fine attention to detail that Bill expends on all aspects of his work – just look at that cast-iron support column and those guttering brackets! The thinness of the roof slates and the slightly peeling timetable also lend real atmosphere to the scene – it's all those barely-registered little details, yet used with just sufficient restraint, that make the difference. And do I need further proof that the *suggestion* of human habitation is infinitely superior to inevitably-flawed attempts at actually portraying it? Photo: Richard Stallwood.

On an end-to-end run, one is forced to collaborate with other people, and for me at least this is where the real enjoyment lies – and with it greater realism. The simple act of running trains in opposing directions can enhance the experience immeasurably. If more people are available, it might be possible to experiment with giving them other roles, in much the way that some of the classic indoor models of the Fifties and Sixties emulated the entire railway, with signalmen, station masters and so on. Giving some one the role of stationmaster/signalman/shunter would be an interesting break from running the trains, and it would reduce the impact on driving of all those other jobs one has to perform. More fancifully, as discussed elsewhere, there is the possibility of having a second person in the role of guard, complete with radio-controlled brakes!

Given this kind of scenario, one can no doubt think of a multitude of other roles that people could play, and features that one could incorporate; for example, working level crossing gates could be little short of a major inconvenience on a solo-operated line (though quite realistic), but would be an interesting feature were someone separate available to open and close them.

As yet, I have never tired of the process of getting a live steamer ready for work; there is a dimension of realism in the rituals one experiences that can never be replicated by the flick of a switch and the turn of the knob of an electric controller. The models look wonderful as they are, but there is no substitute for the way in which they 'wake up' as pressure is raised; what is more, it is a spectacle that seems to appeal to my audience too – truly the real thing made small, and surely worth doing well.

platform is one of pure magic for me. It also seems to create great excitement amongst onlookers. On the LBR, we have enhanced this a little more, by making proper varnished-wood-and-brass train staffs for each section, which can be hung on the transmitter and swapped mid-way.

AN INTERESTING BREAK

Yet here again, I feel that much potential for both enjoyment and realism is often lost; particularly at open days, which after all are the main chance one has to run with multiple drivers, the running of the trains seems more like a grand procession than running a railway. I am often left with the impression that it is more akin to flying model aircraft than replicating a real railway, with all trains running in the same direction (bizarrely, usually anti-clockwise!) and almost no collaboration between drivers beyond that required to keep out of each other's way.

Running more than one train single-handed is a difficult proposition, especially on an end-to-end line, but opportunities really open up when friends come to play… But even at open days, one sees relatively little co-operation of the sort seen here. Two of Andrew Crookell's locomotives double-head an afternoon train back into Castle Bryan on the earlier Lower Bryandale Railway, with each of us at the regulator of one locomotive. This calls for similar concentration as full sized crews needed when double heading, but the satisfaction multiplies by a factor of far more than two.

Rolling stock

Opposite: Roofs are very important on rolling stock, as on buildings. The effort in adding individual planks is more than repaid by the final effect. This uses aero-modelling techniques as its inspiration, and once again, Neil Ramsay got there first…

Above left: Interior detail adds a great deal, even if you do not populate your coaches. This is a Welsh Highland prototype, and was all done from off-cuts of lime and ply – very satisfying. Note the slots to accommodate the 2mm picture glass glazing – another Ramsay technology.

Above right: This interior was more of a challenge – the slats of this L&BR coach were individually cut from mahogany – a job which does rather try the patience as it is hard and tends to split down the grain rather than follow the knife. The finished effect is worth it, though, especially when teamed up with varnished mahogany droplight frames in the windows.

Centre: A Welshpool & Llanfair-inspired van, virtually complete. The metal components were cut from thin brass, drilled and glued in place with superglue. The bolt heads are cut-off household pins. The W-hangers are proprietary, as are the steel wheels, which add valuable weight.

Lower: The van seen earlier, painted and weathered with an airbrush. The lettering was applied using a simple stencil, and then tidied up with a very fine paint-brush. The effect is considerably more realistic than using transfers, not least because the gaps between planks are not covered over using the former method.

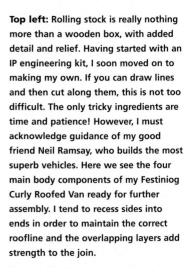

Above: Frets like this do take time, cut from 0.8mm birch ply. The key is light pressure and repeated strokes. This is quite a nice job for a dark evening and for me at least the satisfaction was worth it – even before it went onto the actual vehicle…

Top left: Rolling stock is really nothing more than a wooden box, with added detail and relief. Having started with an IP engineering kit, I soon moved on to making my own. If you can draw lines and then cut along them, this is not too difficult. The only tricky ingredients are time and patience! However, I must acknowledge guidance of my good friend Neil Ramsay, who builds the most superb vehicles. Here we see the four main body components of my Festiniog Curly Roofed Van ready for further assembly. I tend to recess sides into ends in order to maintain the correct roofline and the overlapping layers add strength to the join.

Centre: Obtaining a good paint finish can be difficult. Neil uses aero-modellers' sanding sealer, then car primer, then car aerosols, all sanded down meticulously between coats. I prefer an airbrush for the final coats. This is the CRV again, windows masked out for final spraying. Incidentally, I use an old cotton sheet to achieve the effect of leaded canvas on the roof, stuck in place with a coat of sanding sealer. Slight irregularities in the planks show through delightfully.

Lower: The finished CRV. I must admit that I was not entirely happy with the lining, but this was the first time that I had used a lining pen in anger. What a prototype to choose to start with! No doubt the experts will have spotted the design error – which I realised too late…

S WITH SO MANY THINGS, the issues thrown up by garden railways regarding time period are very different from those of indoor models. Small-scale models built on indoor baseboards exist more clearly in a world of their own. The small size of the models makes it difficult to have the intimate relationship one can have with garden-sized ones; this immediately creates a sense of separation between the modeller and the model, which can be easily extended to the notional time period. In addition, the clear discontinuity created by the baseboard edge means that there is less perceptual mingling between the real world and the modelled one. This means that indoor models either exists in dedicated 'reality capsules' of their own, or conversely, they are portable (so that they take their own reality with them wherever they go).

Contrast this with a garden railway, which much more clearly exists in real space and time. The relatively large scale of the models means that one gets much more closely involved with them, and when it comes to the railways themselves, they are so much bigger than us that they exist around us, and when we run or work on them, we effectively become part of them. This all makes it much more difficult to maintain a 'separation' between reality and the model.

The implications of all this for spatial matters have been discussed quite frequently, but relatively little attention has been

There is little that is explicitly 'period' about this view of *Taliesin* awaiting the 'off' at Queen's Forest Road. The milk churns and gas lamp are about it – though I may judiciously add a few enamel signs when I can source some convincing ones. The train itself, however, is composed of an ornately-lined Victorian locomotive with equivalent rolling stock. To my eyes, the scene portrays a view of ninety years ago in the way that it would have been experienced when it was still 'now'.

given to the aspect of Time. Given that, for the most part, the natural habitat of the steam engine is in the past, how can we convincingly address the issue that ours exist in the Present?

It seems to me that there are three distinct approaches, each of which, well done, can be completely plausible. I will, however, make no pretence that they all convince me equally!

1. IGNORE IT

Perhaps the most common approach is effectively to ignore the issue altogether. The problem may not arise at all if you are mostly just concerned with having fun running your trains. You may attempt some vaguely historical accessories to create a backdrop, but that is about all. Another version of this is to accept that the railway does just exist 'now'. This allows you to

assemble items from any historical period, and is perhaps most compatible with the concept of a model preserved railway. (This also conveniently does away with the geographical contradictions of a disparate collection of motive power and rolling stock). However, this approach also risks ending up looking rather incongruous, with the attendant destruction of atmosphere, and is clearly of limited use to those who are more interested in the whole, authentic railway scene.

2. EMPHASISE IT

The second approach is simply to set a date or era in which your railway will exist, and accept that it will become a period-piece, divorced from real space and time going on around it. In this case, the observer will look in on the model across a 'time threshold', as often happens with indoors modelling. It does, however, allow you to go to town on the period detail, in a way exemplified by Laurie Wright's Cwmcoediog line, which abounds in period paraphernalia hanging outside the shops, people in period costume etc.

Laurie has certainly done a convincing job, but to my mind there always exists the risk of creating a miniature heritage theme park, with the resultant loss of visual realism of a railway that clearly does exist in the present. 'Period' is a strange concept, and in my opinion not entirely connected with the more objective concerns of history. It always makes me feel vaguely uneasy, perhaps because I suspect that we are actually seeing a confected, romanticised version of what once really existed, and partly because to modern eyes it just doesn't look real. I also wonder whether over-restoration is responsible for distorting a real understanding of the past, while you also have to be extremely careful to get it right. For example, while we clearly need to rid ourselves of the perception created by old photographs that

Slowing as it is cautioned by the distant signal, this Londonderry & Loch Swilly 4-8-0 locomotive is hauling a rake of Burtonport Extension coaches. The atmosphere of the period is encapsulated in the train itself, and no doubt connoisseurs of Irish Railways would be able to 'fix' it just on the vehicles shown.

the past existed in black-and-white, I do wonder whether the indiscriminate use of modern paints results in far more garish colour schemes than were actually possible at the time.

3. DOWN-PLAY IT

After much pondering on this issue, I arrived at a Third Way. This was in relation to my own railway, which is notionally set in the first quarter of the Twentieth Century, but which is clearly visible to a wide audience, not just me, and for whom I did not wish to create an overtly 'period' tableau.

My reasoning was this: 'The Past' is simply a confection of the present; it only appears 'period' because we have the benefit of hindsight with which to date it. The styles and technologies of, say, the 1920s appeared just as contemporary, modern even, *at that time* as those of today do to us. Therefore, when viewing what were then new things, the viewer would have had no experience of looking at period technology – while even the historical experience of seeing, for example, High Victoriana would have been tempered by the simple fact that that period was still the relatively recent past. Likewise, the natural world appeared to people at the time exactly as it does now: the trees were just as green in 1920 as they are today, the sun shone in exactly the same way, the wind and rain looked then just as now. In a sense, we are talking about a kind of timelessness, which can still be experienced today – but not, ironically, in

those places that go all-out to create an experience of the past. The place to go is to the countryside. Yes, more subtle changes have taken place even there if you are in the know, thanks to changing farming techniques and Dutch Elm Disease, but in purely aesthetic terms, Nature has not changed, only the technology in the fields. And in the types of area that many of us model, one could be forgiven whether even that is an over-statement.

DISTINCTIVE ASPECTS

Therefore, another approach to encouraging a feel for a given 'era' is actually to underplay almost anything that too explicitly defines any era. I say 'almost' because there are significant exceptions. The other side of this coin is to ensure that you do *not* include anything that would clearly be incongruous, for example people wearing fashions that were clearly too modern, road vehicles or other technologies that post-date your supposed era.

Another mistake made by heritage centres is to over-play their hand. As mentioned earlier, they do this by over-emphasis on the distinctive aspects of a given period at the expense of those things that have provided continuity. What is more, there is also the dilemma of which part of your chosen era one is actually trying to represent: within my chosen 25 years, for example, significant changes took place. (I have exactly the same difficulty with real-life architects and planners who insist on 'period-style' new-build in conservation areas, which in fact were the product of decades or centuries of evolution: exactly *which bit* of 'period' do you try to blend in with?) The only way around this is to specify a very precise date for your model, but at the cost of losing even more of the connection with 'real-time'.

On more mundane level, there has never been a time when everything surrounding us derived from one era. In the Twenties, much everyday material might well have derived from the mid-

Nineteenth Century, just as to day we are still surrounded with products from the past. Thus it becomes completely acceptable to have Victorian artefacts in a Twentieth Century setting, whatever the heritage industry might feel. This was certainly true of NG railways right through the Twentieth Century, and remained true even on the main lines in the U.K. certainly up until the 1970's when significant change finally took place.

However, such items were rarely accorded special attention – they remained everyday objects. Thus, they might not be in particularly good repair, their colours might be muted, and they certainly would not have been found posed in attention-grabbing locations.

So I managed to resolve my period difficulty by accepting that I am trying to model the present day – just a different present day. I am trying to present the first decade of the twentieth century, as it would have appeared to a person at that time, not as it appears to someone today looking back through a century of history.

Therefore, my approach is to under-play almost all of the historical detail, which also has the benefit of removing potential clashes caused when certain items do become incongruous. I have selected certain items such as sack barrows, milk churns (admittedly of Victorian design) seats and lamps that would have existed throughout a long period, but I have ensured that I have chosen nothing that would have appeared *later* than my intended period. This extends to matters such as the colour temperature and brightness of lamps when they come on in the evening – high-intensity modern lighting would shatter the effect.

That way, I can suggest a subtle 'bending' of time, without losing the impression that the railway still exists in the here-and-now. In some ill-defined way, we are looking through Alice's glass into a period characterised by its similarities and continuity with 'Now,' and where the clues to the contrary are subtle and restrained.

But this all changes when a train appears. My major expression of 'period' is the trains themselves – when *Taliesin* runs down the line in its lined-out Victorian maroon, its brass work shining in the sun, and with three suitable coaches in tow, this is the entire *explicit* period feel I find I need...

Botar & Dunmore station in the Ireland of the 1950s. Cavan & Leitrim №8 simmers quietly, while the West Clare diesel railcar (a foreign interloper) waits for non-existent passengers. Another example of a timeless model, where the trains themselves are left to do the speaking... Photo: Neil Ramsay

HOBBIES ARE PECULIAR THINGS. It can be hard to understand why people invest so much time, effort and money in something that, in any wider sense, is an utterly pointless activity. Equally bizarre is the way in which people who are utterly absorbed in their own hobby can fail to appreciate the fervour with which people of a different persuasion follow theirs. Yet, in many ways, we are all the same – the one thing that unites is the almost fanatical passion for some activity that simply ignites a precious spark of recognition in the imagination of the practitioner.

For those of us inside this hobby, matters relating to how and why we make small trains run round lengths of track laid out in our gardens can assume an importance completely out of proportion to the greater significance of the activity. And yet, in a way, such trivial activities actually *are* far more important than they might appear - for contained within them are the records of the significant experiences and values of a unique human life; within those things we do simply for the love of it is captured that which we hold most dear.

Railways exist for what is an apparently mundane purpose: to move people and goods from place to place – but implied within that is a fundamental expression of Man's relationship with this planet: the fact that he finds the need to re-order the Earth to match disparate supply with demand, and in the

Russell calls at Minffordd (LBR). This was only the second season on this part of the line, and it is amazing how quickly the plants have started to create a verdant scene. In the foreground, the water tower is my first experiment with building in real slate. The blocks were sliced up on a wet-wheel tile cutter, and fixed with exterior silicone round a plywood box – a surprisingly therapeutic job, and definitely the way forward for stone buildings. The more I try, the more I come to the conclusion that the best answer is to do things the same way that the original did!

process to create a System that traverses the face of the planet in a unique and complex interaction with every type of climatic and physical environment that it encounters. The labour of a locomotive hauling a train along a track is the culmination of the physical, social, personal, economic and historical circumstance within which that particular railway functioned; the theatrical experience of witnessing the passage of that train the end-product of a highly complex set of interactions.

It can be instructive to witness the reaction of those outside the hobby when its finer points are explained to them. I recall the surprise shown by a friend who had simply not appreciated the diversity of thought and action encompassed by model railways, and who assumed it was a simple matter of handicrafts or 'boys'

toys'. The fact that this hobby can include historical research, artistic composition, social history, horticulture, geographical understanding, aesthetic appreciation and social interaction as well as technical output came as a complete revelation.

MECHANICALLY OR ARTISTICALLY

Railway modelling is clearly about different things to different people, but Peter Jones excellently summed that which we all have in common when he said, "We run trains to recapture something", and in this sense our model making, whether mechanically or artistically inclined, is about something far more significant than a handicraft, namely the expression of a human experience that has particularly moved or affected us, no matter how mysterious the underlying reason for that may be.

It is all too easy to become over-evangelical about one's own interest – indeed that is arguably a defining characteristic of 'The Enthusiast' – but what has become increasingly apparent to me since my accidental arrival in the world of garden railways, is that this approach offers the ultimate potential for expressing all of the things that railways in general mean to me. Listen to the talk amongst any mix of garden railway folk, and I suspect you will hear the same thing, no matter how diverse those outlooks may be. This Cinderella of the wider hobby of railway modelling excels at embodying what a real railway is about in the way that I now feel no indoor model ever can, and for one reason: it employs so many of the real elements that it seeks to recapture. Unlike small scale indoor models, the motive power is often real, the weight of the trains is significant enough to seem real, the construction issues are real - and for me perhaps most significantly of all, the landscapes, times and conditions through which a garden railway runs are *the real thing*. The sun really goes down each day on my railway in a way that can never happen on an indoor model. What is still not fully understood, perhaps, is the way in which reproducing such things in miniature somehow concentrates the experience and distils from it the essential liquor of its being. Why is it that the play of the elements on my model is seemingly more powerful than the original experiences that it evokes, almost a type of heightened reality? Is it the simple effect of selective memory at work, or is it the fact that the act of modelling makes explicit something that was perhaps experienced almost subliminally at the time? Or is it perhaps the shift in relative scale between the observer and the observed that allows us insights that are not possible at full size?

SHOWS OF STEAM

As I write this, the evenings are drawing in, and the clocks will be put back in a couple of weeks' time. The year has been one of significant development on the Lower Bryandale Railway.

The late-afternoon sun illuminates an up train waiting time at Minffordd (LBR). It is quite hard to believe that just nine months before, none of this scene existed, such has been the speed of maturation of the model and the planting. Were it not for the unavoidable intrusion of the fence support, this view would have little that immediately cries 'model' about it. The realism of garden railways at their best is not only uncannily close to full-sized ones, but it also possesses an intangible creative magic all of its own. As a means of expressing our fascination for the real thing, what more could you want?

The railway is quite different now from how it was at the start of the year, and the skills I have developed during its growth have been satisfying to reflect on. Today has been one of those lovely, mellow autumn days, with a golden sun casting its light across our street, the long shadows beautifully accentuating the textures and relief of everything it touched. But of everything, the railway has been the best touched of all. The physical pain of building the chaired, wooden-sleepered track paid for itself today alone, thanks to the wonderful relief in which it was cast; the slate walls' texture stood out at its best, the station building has mellowed to the extent that it looks as though it has always been there. This is not solely about experiencing a railway, but about something that somehow enhances one's experience of the natural process itself. How on earth do you explain that to a non-believer? And yet, the reactions of the usual flow of passers-by, both enthusiast and not, suggested that they were able to share at least part of the experience, the children's excitement at the clear autumn shows of steam in that low sunlight being proof enough that it is not *only* the true believers who can draw pleasure from this hobby.

I am certain that I am not alone in having experienced such days – much garden railway talk is of evocation of the real thing. However, why economise on the experience? I remain bemused by the fact that many railways omit the very ingredients that, for me, would make them special; the standard answer seems to be that their creators deem them not to be necessary – fair enough, perhaps, but I cannot conceive of a railway that would actually be *diminished* by a dose of full-on realism. The architect Mies van der Rohe once said, "God is in the details"; if we omit those details, we are at risk of losing the very defining features of what we seek to recreate – and if we ignore the wider environment of the railway, we risk losing much of what

Another Sunday, another train heading up the Dale with *Taliesin* in charge. Out of sight are probably assorted members of the public, enjoying the unexpected and enchanting spectacle of live steam trains running in an environment they never previously knew was possible. No doubt there will be questions about their provenance, how they work, and how long it all took to make. This line seems to have become real in the eyes of a lot of people round here, and rarely does an hour pass without someone or other leaning over the railings, looking intently at some aspect of the line; not perhaps a level of scrutiny that everyone would be happy with, though I am pleased to say that the vast majority of reaction is complimentary. ('Beautiful' is not uncommonly heard). It's not always apparent what they are looking at – or maybe they are just being inwardly transported, with a little help from me, to somewhere in their imaginations where locomotives such as *Taliesin* still haul narrow gauge trains up winding valleys... Isn't that what it's all about?

the Railway is about in the first place, no matter how absorbing the engineering might be. The imposition of the strict geometry of the railway on the randomness of the earth's surface is a fascinating study in its own right – and one that we can reproduce to perfection in our gardens.

I concede that this is not an easy or quick task; the level of observation, planning and construction is significant – but that is surely to be welcomed as the sign of a maturing hobby, whose practitioners are engaging in a skilled activity. At a time when the sheer physical graft of creating a garden railway is being reduced by the welcome impact of technology and trade support, perhaps now is the time when we should focus less on the compromises forced upon us by our choice of modelling environment and look instead to maximising the sheer magic that can be conjured up by mastering the Art of the garden railway.

Bibliography

Modelling reference

Narrow Gauge Modelling by Peter Kazer, Wild Swan Publications, 2001. Probably my single most referred-to book on all aspects of accurate narrow gauge modelling, even though it is slanted towards the indoor scales.

Historical Railway Modelling by David Jenkinson. Pendragon Publishers, 2001. Again, largely catering for the indoor scales, but a valuable insight into design and operating considerations of real railways.

Fine Scale in Small Spaces: An Approach to model railway design by Iain Rice Wild Swan Publications, 1990. A seminal work on the design of model railways as theatre. Many good ideas that could be applied out of doors.

The Art of Weathering by Martyn Welch. Wild Swan Publications 1993. Again directed at indoor modellers, but still a lot that is applicable, and if nothing else thought-provoking for outdoor modellers too.

Prototype reference

Railway Operation for the Modeller by Bob Essery. ISBN 1 85780 168 7 Midland Publishers, 2003. This deals with standard gauge railways, but is nonetheless excellent for dispelling many modellers' misconceptions of railway operating practices.

The Last Years of the Wee Donegal and *The Last Years of the Wee Donegal Revisited* by Robert Rowbotham Colourpoint Books 1998 and 2002. Even if you don't model Irish railways, the pictures are full of narrow gauge inspiration.

The Welshpool and Llanfair by Ralph I. Cartwright. Rail Romances 2002. Excellent reference source on this characterful line, including the street section in Welshpool and rolling stock diagrams.

The Talyllyn Railway by J.I.C. Boyd. Wild Swan Publications, 1988. Superbly evocative photographs of how the narrow gauge really was in its pre-preservation form. Useful diagrams including obscure details.

Branch Lines Around Portmadoc 1923-46 and *1954-94* by Vic Mitchell and others. Middleton Press 1993 and 1994. More excellent reference material – with the opportunity to compare pre and post preservation scenes. Others in the series, such as that on the Lynton & Barnstaple, are equally useful.

Acknowledgements

That our hobby seems to tap in to such extraordinary goodwill is surely a sign of its worth: people do see it for what it is – a constructive, affirmative and widely appealing way of spending one's leisure. I would like to thank all of the good folk of the garden railway world who have added their bit to the often protracted thought processes of this individual. In particular, the members of the NGGarden email group, who have tolerated the contortions of my pondering with remarkable good humour, and who have always been ready to lend a practical idea when needed. I would also like to thank Peter Hayward, David Halfpenny and George Harris for their encouragement in the early stages of my discovery of the hobby, and Paul Sherwood, Neil Ramsay, Jeremy Ledger, Laurie Wright, Bill Winter, Matthew Labine and Andrew Coward in particular, for their regular doses of inspiration. I would like to thank those people who have provided photos to supplement my own collection in this book, and special thanks are due to Jeremy Ledger for agreeing to write up the section on his masterwork, Tarren Hendre for me. I would also like to thank Gavin Robertshaw for his initial proof-reading of my script.

My railway would also not be the same without the interest of my family and neighbours, who have provided more incentive for action than they might appreciate. And above all, my thanks to my wife Sara; it is my good fortune that she not only tolerates my hobbies but actively encourages and participates in them, and without her support this wonderful if eccentric hobby would probably not have gained the significant place in my life that it has.

Biography

Ian Stock grew up in Somerset, with the combined delights of the last years of WR hydraulics and the early West Somerset Railway for company. He has modelled railways for over thirty-five years, in both 4mm and 2mm scales, before graduating to garden live steam in 2006. Shortly afterwards, he was invited by Mark Found to develop and present The Railway Channel's series *Narrow Gauge in the Garden*, which has been widely seen both online and on DVD. He has also contributed several articles to *GardenRail* and *16MM Today* magazines.

Ian is a schoolteacher by profession and lives in a converted Victorian school in Essex. He is involved from a distance with the restoration of the Lynton & Barnstaple Railway, and his other interests include traditional music, cooking, travel and architecture and design.

Garden Railway Centres

Capel Orchard, London Road, Cheltenham, GL52 6UZ
Tel: 01242 519770
E-Mail: sales@gardenrailwaycentres.co.uk
Web: www.gardenrailwaycentres.co.uk

We supply a full range of items for G Scale and 16mm modellers from Accucraft, Aristo-Craft, Bachmann, Cooper Craft, Hartford, Hillman, LGB, Massoth, Noch, Ozark Miniatures, Peco, Phoenix Sound, Piko, Pola, Preiser, Roundhouse and Woodland Scenics

16mm NGM
www.16mm.org.uk
Join online!

More than 3,000 members worldwide
Friendly network of area groups
Quarterly journal, full of inspiration for the garden railway artist!

LIVE STEAM IN THE GARDEN WITH 16MM NARROW GAUGE MODELLERS
Visit our website or write to the Membership Secretary: Alan Regan, 45, Hollow Wood, Olney, Bucks. MK46 5LZ

MVL BRIDGES

MODEL BRIDGES FOR THE NARROW GAUGE GARDEN RAILWAY

A new range of bridges suitable for many garden railway scales and gauges
SM32, SM45, 16mm Narrow Gauge, 0 Gauge, Gauge 1, G Scale

Aluminium Under Beam, Through Plate Girder, Pony Truss, Bowstring, Inverted Bowstring and Under Arched girder bridge models available to order in various lengths or to your own specifications

| UK NG Freelance Design | Individually Hand Made | Metal finish |
| Bolted & Riveted Construction | Supplied complete less track | |

• *Contact us to discuss your requirements or visit the website*

www.mvlbridges.co.uk
MVL Bridges, 9 Lady Beatrice Terrace, New Herrington, Houghton-le-Spring
Co. Durham DH4 4NE
(0191) 5843181

ROUNDHOUSE

Living Steam Railways
SM32/SM45 & 'G' scale
Established 1982

Just a few models from our wide range of live steam locomotives.

Some of our locomotives are also available as kits where all the hard work is done by us (such as machining and silver soldering), leaving you with a project that is both fascinating and informative. For more information on all of our ready to run Locomotives, Locomotive kits and our vast range of parts, visit our website or telephone us.

Designed, manufactured and tested in Doncaster, England.

Roundhouse Engineering Co. Ltd.
Units 6 to 9, Churchill Business Park, Churchill Rd, Wheatley, Doncaster. DN1 2TF.
01302 328035   www.roundhouse-eng.com   mail@roundhouse-eng.com

Glendale Junction

Suppliers of Garden Railways

ACCUCRAFT
ARISTOCRAFT
BACHMANN
BREKINA

DVD'S & MAGAZINES

Elita

G1MRC
GAUGEMASTER
HELMSMAN
HILLMAN
(Rail Clamps)

JACKSONS MINIATURES
KISS
LGB
Mamod
MASSOTH
MODELBOUW
PECO
PIKO
POLA
PREHM
PREISER
REGNER
ROUNDHOUSE
TRAIN LINE45
TUXCRAFT
(Concrete Products)

"The Complete Garden Railway Experience"

The Shop That Makes The Hobby Fun !!

TRAIN LINE45
Track System
Giving You
Brass & Nickel Track - 2nd, 3rd & 210mm Rad Points
Slow Operating Point Motors
Compatible with Leading Manufacturers

Massoth Decoders, Sound Units etc
Dietz Decoders, Sound Units etc
Supply, Upgrades & Fitting Service

Russ Fragrant Fun

See Our Website For Our Next Live Steam & Digital Running Day
We Welcome...
(or give us a ring)

MasterCard Maestro VISA VISA ELECTRON

Wed - Fri 10.00 am - 5.00 pm
Sat 10.00 am - 4.30 pm
**5 New Row Deeping St James
Peterborough PE6 8NA
Phone 01778 343183**
www.glendalejunction.co.uk
mail@glendalejunction.co.uk

BACK 2 BAY 6

The Craft Village, Mere Park Garden Centre,
Stafford Road, Newport, Shropshire, TF10 9BY

For all your accessories in 1/12th, 7/8th, 16mm & G Scale

Visit: www.back2bay6.net

Email: steve@back2bay6.net

Tel: 01952 820835

READY BUILT AND PAINTED, HAND MADE GARDEN RAILWAY BUILDINGS

FOR 16MM & G SCALE

MADE FROM QUALITY CEMENT USING THE JIGSTONE SYSTEM

ANY BUILDING FROM THE JIGSTONE RANGE OR TO OURS OR YOUR DESIGN

FOR MORE INFORMATION VISIT

www.pdf-models.com
01635 867305

679616

ACCUCRAFT UK LTD
READY TO RUN LIVE STEAM & ELECTRIC LOCOMOTIVES AND ROLLING STOCK FOR GARDEN RAILWAYS

W&L 'Countess' Live Steam

Isle of Man 4 Wheel Coach

'Ragleth' 0-4-0 Live Steam

W&L Goods Van

'Lawley' 0-6-0 Live Steam

L&B 4 Wheel Open Wagon

For Details of our Complete Range of Models Send an A4 SAE To:
ACCUCRAFT UK LTD, PINEWOOD COTTAGE, BROCKHURST,
CHURCH STRETTON, SHROPSHIRE, SY6 6QY.
Or visit our web site at: www.accucraft.uk.com

I P ENGINEERING

**Winterdyne, Spilsby Road,
Eastville, Boston, Lincs. PE22 8JR.**
Phone & Fax: 01205 270373
Visit our secure on-line shop at
www.ipengineering.co.uk

Industrial Loco Kits
What a fantastic choice!

Our range of white-metal and brass industrial loco kits is the finest in the world...probably! Easy to build using epoxy glue or low-melt solder, the kits are complete and come with full instructions; you supply only glue or solder, paint and batteries. Being of metal construction they all 'feel' right and are satisfyingly heavy. No fantastic plastic here!
All kits are available in both 32 and 45mm gauges except the Ruston which is 32mm gauge only.
All kits are **£69.95** each.

Ruston 18/20hp
Lister Petrol
Lister Diesel
Simplex Caravan
Plate Frame Simplex
O&K Midget

Post & packing free on all UK orders over £250. Otherwise see our catalogue or website for p&p charges. Phone for a FREE catalogue.

**All major credit cards accepted by post,
phone and secure on-line shop, UK or Export**
MasterCard VISA

Jackson's Miniatures
www.jacksonsminiatures.com
Affordable and adaptable garden railway building kits

Large station (based on Raven Square on the Welshpool & Llanfair Light Railway)
Kit - £55.00 Textured sheet pack - £40.00
when ordered at the same time as the kit
(normal price £47.92)

Signal Box (based on Castle Caereinion on the Welshpool & Llanfair Light Railway)
Kit - £30.00 Textured sheet pack - £15.50
when ordered at the same time as the kit
(normal price £18.38)

Waiting Room (based on Castle Caereinion on the Welshpool & Llanfair Light Railway)
Kit - £19.50 Textured sheet pack - £7.75
when ordered at the same time as the kit
(normal price £9.19)

Country station
Kit - £32.50 Textured sheet pack - £25.00
when ordered at the same time as the kit
(normal price £29.95) (Weatherboarding and slate or corrugated roof)

Our garden railway building kits are machine cut from moisture proof mdf and are intended for permanent outdoor use. The kits include our fine detail styrene doors and windows and comprehensive instructions. Decorative plastic sheeting is available separately. Please see our web site for full details of these and all our other products. Our doors and windows are available separately – perfect for scratch builders!

Old Fir Tree Inn, Peacemarsh, Gillingham, Dorset SP8 4EU
tel: 01747 824851 e-mail: sales@jacksonsminiatures.com fax: 01747 821405

MARTIN'S MODELS *Garden Railways*

G SCALE & 16MM MODELS, U.K. SOLE AGENTS FOR REGNER LIVE STEAM ENGINES

Regner steam engines are all excellent value for money. Priced from £219, most are suitable for 32 and 45mm track and are well-engineered to give years of service. The geared range includes "Chaloner" de Winton, "Victoria", a scale model of a loco which ran on the Plynlimon & Hafan tramway, "Lumberjack" a logging engine, an 8-ton Shay, "Vincent", an overtype engine with chain drive and the well-known "Willi" and "Konrad". Their "posh" engines are engineering masterpieces! I keep in stock the highly-detailed **Accucraft/BMS** rolling stock and engines at discounted prices. Also **Peco track** in 32 and 45mm gauges and offer a discount for quantity. We also sell **Roundhouse** loco's and normally have one or two in stock. The **Bachmann** range now includes **Thomas & His Friends** - super large scale and good value.

Established almost 20 years, our aim is to give value, unbiased advice and good service.

**Martin's Models, Hatton Gardens, Kington, Herefordshire HR5 3RB
Tel: 01544 230777, fax 01544 231600**